Hugh Hefner's First Funeral And Other True Tales Of Love And Death In Chicago

Pat Colander

CONTEMPORARY
BOOKS, INC.
CHICAGO

Library of Congress Cataloging in Publication Data

Colander, Pat.
  Hugh Hefner's first funeral, and other true tales of
love and death in Chicago.

  1. Crime and criminals—Illinois—Chicago—Case studies.
2. Chicago (Ill.)—Social conditions—Case studies.
I. Title.
HV6795.C4C55   1985   364.1'09773'11   85-2635
ISBN 0-8092-5545-6 (pbk.)

Some of these stories appeared in other forms in the
Chicago *Reader.* I would like to thank the *Reader* for
permission to reprint those portions.   —P.C.

Untitled poem on pages 4 and 5 reprinted by permission of
Farrar, Straus, and Giroux, Inc. From *Even Tide* by Larry
Woiwode, copyright © 1970, 1971, 1977 by Larry Woiwode.

Published by Contemporary Books, Inc.
180 North Michigan Avenue, Chicago, Illinois 60601
Manufactured in the United States of America
Library of Congress Catalog Card Number: 85-2635
International Standard Book Number: 0-8092-5545-6

Published simultaneously in Canada by Beaverbooks, Ltd.
195 Allstate Parkway, Valleywood Business Park
Markham, Ontario L3R 4T8 Canada

4

Contents

To my grandmother,
Mary Elizabeth Connors

Hugh Hefner's First Funeral And Other True Tales Of Love And Death In Chicago

Introduction

FUGITIVES

When I was very small it seemed to me that everyone was a fugitive. There was a local news program that ran mug shots of people on the FBI's most-wanted list—scary-looking men with three-day-old beards and deep, dark pockets under their eyes—as a daily public service. I knew that the mother of two of my playmates had had a number stamped on her arm when she was in a Nazi concentration camp in Poland.

On my way to morning kindergarten, I saw two plainclothes cops sitting in a car in front of a house across the street from mine. Even the kids in the neighborhood knew that the guy who lived there was in the Mob.

You had better vote Democratic, I learned, because if you didn't, your garbage would not be picked up and you would never get a job. Or worse, you might be taken to the torture chamber in the basement of the alderman's house.

There were spies everywhere.

Thus I discovered the regional original sin born on Chicago's souls. Town citizenship required you to have something to hide, even if it was only your light under a bushel basket. The early realization that nothing is quite what it appears to be had a profound effect. Not that I disbelieved everything I was told; I was just cautious. I developed what would become a lifelong habit of studying gestures, hairdos, figures of speech, modes of dress, and tones of voice for verification of what was actually being said. My suspicions made me curious, and I was drawn to stories I believed to be real. Erle Stanley Gardner's Perry Mason books and John Steinbeck's novels attracted me. My perverse nature, I found, could be put to some good use. European monks had saved civilization by copying down everything they knew. I could do the same through these Dark Ages and grow up slightly less confused.

Chicago defensiveness, I discovered, had its nuances. The city craved recognition though it did not think much of its accomplishments. And it had a fantasy that, collectively, it was more straightforward and direct than most other places.

The fact that the town is such a braggart, that it has a genius for self-promotion, has always given a slant to Chicagoans' exaggerations and their view of local history. How did a city develop this personality, this heart of paranoid insecurity covered by indecent, loud-mouthed swagger? Some say it was because Chicago's birth was so violent. Perhaps the city never really got over the shock of incorporation 150 years ago, coming on the heels of the swell, a population that had doubled in size, energy, diversity, and corruption in just a few years. I like to think, however, that this Second City voodoo—our preference for a vile nature and reputation over next-best status—was always in the aura of the place.

Our choice of identity had a prehistoric quality to it. It is a primitive, but ingenious, mentality that sizes itself up using volume as the only criterion for greatness. Maybe our forefathers knew that striving for real achievement was too painful and lengthy a process. Better to grab the berth no one wanted: the most unholy climate, the rankest charlatans, the greediest thieves, the most vicious gangsters, most blatant liars, and most amateurish culture. Better to deny a thing has any merit at all, if it is not the best.

I think Chicago's ambiance has always had a special appeal for a certain type of person amused by a Sisyphean struggle, a person who wants to be part of a losing tradition. Chicago is populated with people who think it's funny.

And so I came to believe that rawness had virtue, and madness—as long as it was true madness—made, as Emily Dickinson said, divinest sense.

AGITATORS

for Paul Tyner

Tonight if I had in me nine-tenths of my life, I'd
Get up on this barstool and I'd dive on a knife.
Oh, it helps to—Haw! Oh, I've offended my
Friends and my family, too, with my brag
And nastiness, performed after two
A.M. over long-distance lines.

It helps to be oiled to be honest, Bub.
Bring me another drink.

When I'm drinking I don't like to wash,
And that's lobster you smell.
And if you don't like it, lady,
Then you and your nose can both go to hell.

Oh, it helps to be oiled to be honest, yes,
Bring me another drink.

Once at a party on Sutton Place
I bumped a big canvas off a wall
And told the hostess what I thought of her face,
Well, my flying coat tackled me in the elevator hall.

Oh, I've shouted so loud children have shivered!
I've sung so off-key I was ashamed!

4

Introduction

I've lied about my marriageable status,
My income, my age, my business, my name!

I've spilled drinks and broken glasses,
Passed out on the floor all night
And pissed it, dropped hot ash over her dresses
And been helped by her in unsuccessful fights.

Oh, it pays *to be oiled to be honest!*
Bring me another drink!

Last night I kicked her in the ribs and on a run
Blew my cookies down the dishes in the sink,
Seeing in Technicolor rushes what I'd become,
Or was to her, a walking-talking Spiritual Stink.

I have to be oiled to be honest,
So bring me another drink, please,
As I close this on this rainy day in
This roadside bar up north of Kalamazoo,
By apprising you all, family and ex-friends,
Of how I'm about as happy with me as you. Amen.

An untitled poem from *Even Tide* by Larry Woiwode

Though I was intellectually aware that craziness could be terribly dangerous, the first time this had any real emotional impact on me was the day Paul Tyner made an all-out effort to kill himself. Paul Tyner was already pushing it to the limit when I met him at the end of 1974. He was always wildly drunk and often brilliantly funny. Though he was a gifted mathematician who worked off and on at some of the universities around town and for IBM, "How You Play the Game," a short story published in the *New Yorker* in 1968 had won an O. Henry prize, and he had elongated the story into a stark, existential novel called *Shoot It*. When I met him he had just returned from New York, where David Susskind and George C. Scott were making a movie out of the book.

Paul Tyner had held together despite his drinking bouts for a good many years by then. He had been at the University of Illinois in Champaign in the '60s, part of a crowd that included Larry Woiwode, who would become a formidable novelist, and Roger Ebert, then editor of the school newspaper and now a well-known film critic. The group hung around the Capitol, a saloon in Champaign, and then they started to graduate and move to Chicago. Somebody was vaguely related to Willie Kilkarrey, an elfin, platinum-haired Irishman who owned a tavern on the west side of Wells Street, north of North Avenue, in Chicago's Old Town neighborhood, and so the crowd from the Capitol ended up at O'Rourke's. In the early '70s, the neighborhood was gritty and camp and loaded with action. Old Town was a haven for runaways, ex-cons, dopers, punks, and the politically disenfranchised, as well as anybody who wanted to call himself an artist. Wells Street's seediness had a certain charm, even in the sickly odor of the summer air, marijuana, and incense wafting over prairie and parking lot dust. Paddy Bauler, ward committeeman alderman extraordinaire, and king of the neighborhood, had once roamed the street.

Old Town was loaded with bars and restaurants and tourist traps. Second City, a ramshackle cabaret theater which had been started about fifteen years earlier by a group from the University of Chicago, was thriving. Piper's Alley—which really was an alley, although the winding corridor was made of brick rather than concrete—had grown up next door to the theater. The arcade started at a pizzeria and wound back through a cavelike tunnel that ended with a candy store and the stairway to the Aardvark Theater, a movie house that featured what were then known as "art films." Directly across the street was The Earl of Old Town, a showcase for wandering minstrels singing the songs of the disaffected.

North Avenue between Larrabee and Clark was open and spacious, really a traditional Chicago boulevard, with a wide island of pavement bisecting the street. On the south side of the street, across from O'Rourke's, the Earl, Second City, and Piper's Alley, was the Old Town Ale House. It catered to a rougher trade. Maureen Munson, during one of her periods out of the local mental institution, had painted the faces of the regular customers on the east wall inside the tavern. Paul Tyner's picture was large, unmistakable, and near the center.

His drunken escapades were legendary by 1975. With the money he made from the book he rented a Rolls Royce and a chauffeur and purchased a wardrobe of paisley ties and suits with wide lapels. He had insulted important people, outraged women, and driven off a wife and two children. Everyone knew a Paul Tyner story: The last day at a computer job, he had called his boss and said his balls had turned to brass and they were too heavy to drag into the office. Under arrest for public intoxication, he had asked to make his single phone call and ordered a pizza.

By 1975, the money had run out, he was unable to hold a job, and most of the bars refused to serve him. He was living on the couches of friends who would still tolerate him. He had established a pattern of sobering up long enough to write a review for *Playboy* magazine, collect his fee, and spend it on booze.

The morning before the day he tried to kill himself, he had written an article on a borrowed typewriter, dressed in a suit and tie, and gone to the magazine offices. That afternoon I ran into him on the corner. He was staggering and nonsensical, raving about the fact that no one would sell him a drink. He said, if I wouldn't get him any booze, I could at least let him use the bathroom, so I let him into my apartment. I was secretly hoping he was out of it enough to pass out. Instead, he fell facedown on a glass-topped coffee table. It shattered into a hundred pieces and made a deep cut in one of his arms. I wrapped his arm, which was bleeding badly, in a bath towel, all the while insisting I should take him to the hospital a couple of blocks away. Somehow he found a mop and a bucket and began wiping the blood off the floor. The towel was soaked, and I was frantic. I threatened to call an ambulance. He protested. If he went to the hospital, he said, they would lock him up. I went to the phone. When I looked up he was gone. Later I heard he had straightened out enough to get served, continued to drink for a few more hours, and crashed on someone's living room floor.

Twenty-four hours went by before someone noticed that Paul had not moved a muscle in all the time he had been asleep. Then somebody else discovered several empty bottles of pills—pills he had been given by various doctors to steady his nerves through attempts at quitting booze. An ambulance was called, and he was taken to the hospital. His pulse was almost nonexistent, his blood pressure was very low, and he was in a coma. Somehow he lived through it. When he woke up, the doctor in charge of the alcoholic unit told a few of us friends that, since nobody knew how to get in touch with his family, we had a choice: we would have to take turns sitting with him or Paul would be released. Paul would be going through detoxification, he explained, and he could not afford to keep a nurse with him all the time.

I began my first shift the next afternoon. Paul was awake and alert, although subdued. The large, bald doctor was standing at his bedside, screaming insults at him. Not only was he worthless, he was also diabolical, the doctor said. The physician irritated me. I had seen Paul Tyner inflict plenty of damage, but it was mostly damage to himself. Paul was not a dumb person. I could not see how scolding and berating him would help matters. But Paul Tyner and this doctor understood each other and alcoholism better than I understood anything, as it turned out.

When the doctor left I laid some books I had brought on the table. For the first time, I noticed that Paul's hands and feet were tied to the metal sides of the bed with wide leather straps. We chatted for a few minutes about something innocuous. Then he looked me in the eye and asked me to please untie him. I said I couldn't.

"Why?" he asked in an even, sensible voice. "Do you enjoy seeing me helpless like this?"

I shook my head. I was frightened. He seemed so utterly normal.

"What are you doing here, anyway?" he demanded. "You don't know me. You're not my friend. You just want to look at me."

I sat down in a chair by the window. He started to pull on the leather straps and thrash around, all the time yelling at me, insulting me, searching through his memory for my weaknesses, trying to get me to hate him just enough to turn him loose. I sat motionless and stared into the dark street. After about an hour, he quieted for a while, then he started up again. I was there for six hours before the next person came to relieve me. His tirade had worked in the sense that I was totally exhausted and very upset. I thought I would have let him go if I hadn't been utterly certain that releasing him was tantamount to killing him.

Three years went by before I saw him again. He had returned to his mother's home in New Jersey, become very active in Alcoholics Anonymous, and had a lucrative job as a resident wizard at a computer design firm. He came to Chicago on a visit on his way to a new job in San Francisco. Paul haunted his old hangouts and tried to pick up girls, though he usually spent the night on my couch. One evening Larry Woiwode came over and took Paul and me back to his house in the suburbs for dinner. Larry read the poem he had written for Paul aloud and asked Paul if he would mind if it was dedicated to him. Perhaps, pestered by his own demons, Larry had returned to his Christian roots, and Paul mentioned a similar experience during the time he lived with his mother. Larry also read from the Bible and a passage from a novel he was working on. Larry's wife's parents showed up, and Paul got into a spirited conversation with her father about his business, which was coffin-making.

When Paul got to California he wrote me a thank-you note, which I did not answer.

In the summer of 1983, I heard that Paul Tyner was dead. I called the coroner in Los Gatos, California, who said that Paul had died August 9, 1983. He had blown his head off with a heavy caliber rifle in the bathroom of his home. His two sons, now teenagers, had been in the next room. The official said he had released the body to a local undertaker, so I called him. Paul had been cremated; the undertaker and one of the sons had scattered the ashes somewhere around there.

Paul Tyner had been a very important person, I explained to the undertaker. He had written a book and won an O. Henry prize. He was a mathematical genius, I said.

The undertaker said he was sorry. Nobody told him who Paul Tyner was.

SURVIVORS

I recently came to the conclusion that this psychotic need for attention, even the wrong kind of attention, which I had always associated with this town, has spread like a bad spill. And though I still understand the joke about the lazy, frustrated Chicagoan trying desperately to be the very worst he can be, I no longer think it's so funny.

One morning not long ago, on my way to the corner drugstore to pick up newspapers, I was intercepted by a camera crew and a television reporter. They were taking pictures of a middle-aged man in a motor-driven wheelchair and a small, elderly woman using a metal cane to walk alongside him. The young reporter asked me if I knew what had happened. She explained that a woman who lived in the high-rise building three doors from my house had been abducted from in front of her building at about 5:00 A.M., taken to a house on the far south side—as it happened, in the block where my father grew up—and raped by twenty men. How long had I lived in this area, this hopelessly effervescent journalist wanted to know.

Four years.

"Do you consider this a safe neighborhood?" I could not answer her question. "Well, what's safe at five o'clock in the morning?" she prodded hopefully. By this time, the large man with a camera on his shoulder had turned around to face me. "Could we interview you?" the woman asked. I shook my head from side to side and waved my hand in front of my face, as though I were the owner of some shady business, suddenly confronted by Mike Wallace. As I ran away, I heard the cameraman say, "It won't hurt."

Though it becomes more difficult all the time, you can still walk, run, or move away from television reporters. But you cannot avoid madness, or drug addiction, or alcoholism, or violence, or anger, or stupidity by moving to another neighborhood or another city. Craziness, I have decided, is not really a function of regionalism anymore. Later that day, as though to prove this, while the Democrats were at a podium in San Francisco extolling the virtues of family life, inherited values, and hard work, a lunatic from Ohio, a husband and father, marched into a family restaurant in a San Diego suburb and shotgunned twenty-one people to death before a sharp-shooting police officer could put an end to him.

Later, I'm sure, there was a television reporter in San Ysidro, California, asking someone who lived three doors from the McDonald's if she considered it a safe neighborhood. Of course, had she said yes, she would have been wrong. None of us lives in a safe neighborhood. We cannot guard ourselves against gun-toting maniacs at the hamburger stand any more than we can prevent their widows from trying to sell their stories.

We have adjusted to pervasive insanity as effectively as if our bodies had evolved a biological tolerance to toxic levels of carbon dioxide.

In fact, we have adjusted to craziness too well. The madness we no longer find amusing we ignore. And there is something very wrong about that. Because what we ignore we will forget. When loss of memory becomes standard, lunacy is separated from context, and without context, there is nothing to check its growth. Where sickness is rampant, health becomes obscure, hidden, even undesirable. Inevitably it reaches everyone. Whole societies have gone crazy this way and eventually have been destroyed. All because they forgot to remember.

So the stories in this book are memories—tales of people reacting to love, outrage, illness, or despair. The situations, the contexts, are recognizable and human; the reactions may be a bit less easy to identify—they range from death, loss of mind, and spiritual transformation to a flinch, a grimace, or a vague recognition that things will never be the same. But the reactions are there, standing out in a proper light for examination. They are stories that I think are significant because, even where there is no adequate explanation, there is shape, color, and form to the violence or eccentricity that may otherwise seem random.

But most of all, these stories, bits of history preserved, have survived; these are the witnesses. They mark the spot where the sparrow fell, where the door closed, where the survivors stood before they moved on.

1

Love And Death In Chicago

The Giangrandes, at first glance, were a classic middle-class couple: five kids, two Chevy Novas, a brick bungalow with a picture window and a chain-link fence. Michael Giangrande, the son of Italian immigrants, worked long hours at a factory near his house, and he and his wife saved their money and dreamed of good educations and better lives for their children. But their dream was deferred, run off the track by the demons that lurked beneath the surface. Pat and Mike could not avoid the past, their mistakes, their brush with the everyday insanities. As much as they wanted to be part of the mainstream, as much as they wanted to be the all-American family, as much as they thought that material things would mask their failings and insecurities, they were not strong enough at the broken places. And one night in August 1979 the bubble burst. Behind the placid exterior of their house near Midway airport, muffled by the churning of the air conditioner, something terrible happened to the Giangrande family.

Robert Kooy grows soybeans on a farm about a quarter-mile south of the highway that marks the dividing line between Will County and Kankakee County. On the morning of Sunday, August 26, 1979, Kooy and his wife were on their way to church—about 9:30—when they noticed two cardboard boxes sitting in a field near a north-south road that intersects the highway. Kooy opened the larger box, which was sealed with masking tape; finding that it contained parts of a human body, he returned to his house and called the police.

Ed Jackson was already at church, in the nearby town of Bourbonnais, when he was notified about five minutes later of the discovery at the Kooy farm. At about 9:50, Jackson arrived at the site, where he and other Kankakee County police officers proceeded to take pictures, make measurements, draw diagrams, and search the area for evidence of what they were pretty sure was a homicide. Other than the two boxes, both of which contained body parts, they found nothing out of the ordinary at the Kooy farm. This work took about an hour.

Wes Wiseman, the Kankakee County coroner, showed up, put the boxes in a fire department ambulance, and drove them to Saint Mary's Hospital in Kankakee. Jackson and one of the patrolmen followed the ambulance, while another policeman remained at the scene to poke around some more. While Jackson was en route to the hospital, the officer who'd stayed behind called him on the radio to tell him that he'd found some more stuff on the other side of the road. Jackson returned to the scene and found a grocery bag from the Colony Foods store, a store he knew was part of a Chicago chain, and a large, clear plastic bag containing a laundry detergent box; the detergent box, in turn, contained other plastic bags covered with blood. The policeman took more photographs and measurements and drew another set of diagrams before they took the stuff away with them. They requested that the Illinois State Police make an aerial search, and the state cops obliged about an hour later, looking over a three-mile area. But they found nothing.

By midday, everybody had assembled back at the morgue at Saint Mary's in Kankakee. Jackson and the patrolman who'd helped him were joined by police sergeants Bill Marks and Tim Nugent. Sheriff William Scroggins, Patrolman Jerry Pippin, and three deputy coroners were in the room when Jackson, Marks, and Wiseman started to unload the boxes. The smell wasn't too bad, which made them think that the boxes hadn't been sitting around very long. The weather had been warm. The larger box, a toilet-paper carton with the words "Pine Grove Motel" hand-lettered in magic marker on its side, contained a plastic bag with a woman's torso clad in a blood-soaked nightgown that had once been beige. In the other box, which had once held bags of potato chips, there were plastic bags containing a head—minus its upper dental plate—a pair of legs, and arms without hands. The police took pictures of all the parts, pieced the body back together as well as they could, and measured it. Then the body and the bloody evidence were put into a cooler at the morgue.

A teletype went out at about 1:15 that afternoon, asking if anybody knew of a Pine Grove Motel; or of a white female, five feet two inches to five feet five inches tall, about forty years old, with brown hair and blue or blue-green eyes, who had been reported missing; or of a pair of hands, possibly wrapped in a clear plastic bag.

●   ●   ●

By Sunday night, Geraldine Giangrande was getting worried about her son Michael and his family. When Michael called on Friday he sounded tired and upset. When she saw him on Saturday, at his house on the southwest side of Chicago, he told her that his wife, Pat, had gotten angry with him late Thursday night; she'd packed some clothes and stormed out of the house. Geraldine Giangrande didn't know that Pat had a history of disappearing for a few days whenever she got angry with Michael or the kids. Nor was she aware that Pat had frequently run away from her second husband—run away to Michael, before they were married. Michael Giangrande, who was Pat's third husband, had no more of an idea about where she went than Ed Norris, her second husband, had had when she had left him. Michael claims he knew that sometimes she returned to Ed Norris, sometimes she went to a nearby motel, and on other occasions she went to stay with a relative or with girlfriends. But she always came back within a few days. The fact that she was gone was less disconcerting to Michael than the angry explosion that punctuated her departure. Geraldine Giangrande knew that Michael had gone driving around, looking for his wife's car, for a few hours Saturday night. She also knew that Michael figured Pat would return home sometime Sunday. Sunday was Pat's birthday, and while Michael was out looking for her car on Saturday night, he stopped and bought her a birthday card.

Geraldine Giangrande was puttering around the five-room apartment in Evergreen Park that she shared with her husband, Vito, when she heard something about a woman's body found near Kankakee. She was listening to the television with half an ear, not really watching it, and by the time she got interested in the news item it was over. She made a mental note, got into bed, and went to sleep.

There was a story in the Monday morning *Chicago Tribune* that said a dismembered body had been found; it mentioned the Colony Food bag and the "Pine Grove Motel" label on the box. The article said "the woman's body was bruised either from a beating or from the dismemberment" and that police were hoping to learn the woman's identity and establish a motive for the killing.

●   ●   ●

At 11:00 A.M., the Kankakee authorities moved the dismembered body from the cooler at the hospital to a room at the Fitzpatrick Funeral Home. Officers Jackson, Nugent, and Marks were there, along with Patrolman Pippin and representatives of the coroner's office. Joseph Ambrozich was there representing the crime lab, a part of the Illinois Department of Law Enforcement Support Services Division, and after the autopsy he would take all the physical evidence to the laboratory in Joliet for a lot of different tests. Dr. Edward Shalgos, a pathologist from Frankfort, Illinois, performed the autopsy. First, Dr. Shalgos asked that photographs of identifying marks—like the birthmarks on the back and neck—be taken. After he washed the head, close-up color photos of the face and of a bandage on the left toe were shot. The pictures of the face would later be used to identify the body. Dr. Shalgos checked to make sure the victim was not pregnant. Her hair was naturally brown, he said to everyone in the room, and she had hazel eyes. Dr. Shalgos continued to poke and prod, cut and peel away, announcing his findings as he went along. The victim was in her early thirties, he said. She weighed about 155 pounds. There were no signs of sexual abuse at either the rectum or the vagina, and he doubted that she had been raped, but he used cotton swabs to take smears from both areas so Ambrozich could check them under a microscope in Joliet. The woman had eaten breakfast food before her death, including a bit of peach or nectarine. Dr. Shalgos estimated the time of death as somewhere between Friday morning and Friday evening, about ninety minutes after the victim had eaten. One of the police officers asked what type of tools were used to dismember the body. Shalgos said he thought the flesh had been cut to the bone with a knife and that an electric or gas-driven power saw was then used to sever the bones. Dismemberment had occurred shortly after death, he speculated, very likely two days before the body was found and placed in the cooler. It looked like the victim had had children, although at the time of her death she was wearing an intrauterine device. He removed from her uterus the IUD, and it was secured as evidence. Ambrozich collected his samples. He had difficulty getting blood, however, because there was so little left in the body.

In his written report, Shalgos described the information he had and the physical evidence he had found.

> . . . Further information then obtained from Coroner's record and investigator indicates finding at 0900 by farmer and wife of two boxes in ditch, stating variably content of upper torso, and head-arms-legs, the legs also separately cut at knees, the hands missing, and a question raised of bullet wound of face-head, some lower teeth noted present but all upper missing together with absence of dentures, dew on ground

but boxes completely dry to suggest realtively recent deposit at finding site. At some distance from the above finding, a third box was also found which originally contained All detergent, and currently contained bloodied large plastic bags, a pair of dishwashing type bloodied rubber gloves, and a baby's T-shirt size six; the torso component was in a beige nightgown, and a question of rape is raised although no reason stated; a grocery bag was also noted with printing "Colony Foods," being a chain-store in the Chicago area.

The facial wound, Shalgos wrote, was not made by a bullet:

. . . traumatic abnormality appearing minor and irrelevant and in part postmortem inclusive of a right scalp adynamic laceration except for a penetrating rather circular laceration of right face-head extending into maxillary sinus but no further, with bullet identity-origin excluded; no internal components, and no natural abnormality demonstrated, and no residual body fluids except for gastric content pasty-digestate with some nectarine identity only. . . . Death is of unknown cause at this time, and toxicology does not appear promising in view of absence of body fluids, but certificate completion will be deferred pending the latter results.

Shalgos was right. Ambrozich was unable to determine the cause of death.

●   ●   ●

Geraldine Giangrande read about the "Pine Grove Motel" in the newspaper and thought it was familiar; she tried to call her son, but the line was busy. About 1:00 in the afternoon, she called the Evergreen Park police and told an officer there that she had read a description of a dead woman found near Kankakee and she was afraid that the woman might be her daughter-in-law. Jackson received a call from the Evergreen Park police at about 3:00 P.M. The Evergreen Park officer relayed Mrs. Giangrande's story to Jackson. Jackson called Geraldine Giangrande, who had, in the meantime, reached her son, who had confirmed the fact that his wife Pat had taken a box with the words "Pine Grove Motel" written on the side when she left the house early Friday morning. Mrs. Giangrande told this to Jackson.

"We were talking back and forth," Geraldine Giangrande said of the conversation. "He asked if she had pierced ears. I said, 'Yeah, she had pierced ears.' He asked me if she had jewelry on. I said, 'No, no jewelry on.' He asked if she could have been raped. I said I didn't know. . . 'maybe I should have my son call you.' " Jackson said that Mrs. Giangrande told him about the box, also about the Thursday night argument and her daughter-in-law's subsequent disappearance. He noted that she became too upset to talk or give him any more information. When Geraldine Giangrande called Michael back, a patrolman from the Chicago Police Department was with Michael, making out a missing-person report. The Chicago policeman called Jackson from Michael Giangrande's home. Michael got on the phone with Jackson. Yes, his wife did wear an upper dental plate and shopped at the Colony Foods store near their home. Michael Giangrande's description of his wife matched the victim, though he guessed his wife was a few years younger and twenty pounds lighter than the police had estimated the dead woman.

"When is your wife's birthday?" Jackson asked.

"August 26," Michael replied.

"What year?"

"I don't know," Michael admitted. He began to cry. "We've been married seven years, and I don't know her exact birthday. I don't know exactly how old she is." Michael gave Jackson the name and address of his wife's dentist and promised to drive downstate that evening to look at the pictures of the dismembered woman and determine if she was, in fact, his wife. He immediately set off for Kankakee with Laura Diane, his wife's fifteen-year-old daughter by her second marriage. The Kankakee police called Patricia Giangrande's dentist and described her mouth to him. He said that it sounded familiar and that he would come to Kankakee that night to see if he could help with the identification. Michael and Laura Diane stopped once to call the Kankakee police station and ask directions, because they had lost their way.

That night, Mrs. Giangrande watched the six o'clock news on Channel 2 and heard John Drummond give this report: "The torso found in Kankakee County is the sixth dismembered body to turn up in the Chicago area in the last sixteen months. On August 5, the torso of a man was found in the northwest suburb of Barrington Hills.

"Last year, the dismembered bodies of two males and two females were found in remote sections of Cook County.

"One torso, a male, was discovered on September 21, 1978, in a forest preserve near Calumet City. A female victim was found August 22 in a steamer trunk in Calumet City. On June 21, the torso of a female was found in the canal near Lemont. And on April 30, 1978, the remains of the first torso victim were discovered in the Skokie Lagoons.

"The cut-up remains of the latest victim was found in a soybean field about sixteen miles northeast of Kankakee. The body was in two boxes that lay side by side. Authorities were unable to find the woman's hands and dental plate.

"Authorities say there is no evidence to connect any of the grisly slayings, but they note that in all six cases the victims were murdered elsewhere and their remains dumped in remote areas. None of the murders has been solved and only one of the victims, a twenty-one-year-old Hammond woman, has been identified."

Michael and Laura Diane arrived at the Kankakee sheriff's police headquarters at about the same time the news program went on the air. Michael was given color photographs of the victim's head, and moments later he identified these as pictures of his wife, Patricia. He fell apart.

●   ●   ●

Right away on Thursday morning she had started in on Woody. As Michael Giangrande tells it, he and Pat were expecting the Lakomiaks for dinner, and Pat wanted the house spotless. The kids—Laura Diane, Woody (also called Michael, Jr.), Binky (whose real name was Adrian), and Lisa—began cleaning in the morning. Woody, the thirteen-year-old, was scrubbing the stove in the kitchen. Michael, who was on vacation from work that week, went out and did the shopping. Pat was planning to serve Chicken Kiev made in the microwave, a recipe she had been using for about a year. She had gotten a lot of compliments on that Chicken Kiev. By afternoon, the place was shaping up—except for the sink and the stove top. Woody's jobs.

When Michael got home from the store the situation was beginning to get out of hand. If Woody couldn't get the spots off the range, Pat suggested, they would have to throw the stove top away and get a new one. OK, Michael said. Trying to appease her, he called Imperial Kitchen & Baths, the appliance store on Pulaski where he had originally purchased the stove. "Where can I get a new top for the stove?" Michael asked the salesman. "Mine's dirty."

"A new top!" the salesman said. "You can't buy a new top."

"Then I want a new stove," Michael said. "But I want to get it tonight."

"You're crazy," the salesman replied. "There's no way you can get it tonight. It'll take a week to come." Pat Giangrande didn't want a clean stove top in a week. "If we don't get that stove clean, we're just going to have to call the Lakomiaks up and tell them not to come," she screamed. "They're expecting a dinner out, and they're going to end up making dinner for themselves." Woody scrubbed. Michael prepared the chicken for the microwave. Pat lost her temper. She kicked Woody in the ribs. Michael decided that the best idea was to get Woody out of his mother's sight so she would calm down and forget about the damn stove top. He phoned Joe and Adeline Lakomiak to say that he would pick them up soon, figuring to get the laundry he had dropped off in the morning on the same trip. When Mike and Woody left it was about six o'clock.

They returned with the wash and the Lakomiaks about an hour later. The Giangrande home was the picture of tranquility. The four girls—including Andrea, the baby—were cleaned up for dinner, and Pat was ready to receive her guests. Laura Diane mixed a screwdriver for Joe. Pat was drinking, which was fine with Michael—he thought she was her funniest, most sociable self when she'd had a few. Michael may have had a drink or a beer that night—he doesn't remember—but he doesn't really care for booze that much. He is a slight man and can't hold it, he says. Pat had known Mrs. Lakomiak longer (they met when Pat worked briefly at the A&P meat-packing plant in 1971), but Pat really enjoyed talking to Joe. She liked to talk about high finance, the economy, money. "It was just like my wife," Mike says. "She ain't got a pot to piss in, but she has all these ideas about how to invest money and all these opinions about the price of gold and silver." The Chicken Kiev was a hit, and the kids cleared the table, put the dishes in the dishwasher, and went away. The adults drank some more, talked, and had coffee. Later, the big kids put the little kids to bed. Woody and Laura Diane parked in front of the television set. The Giangrandes drove the Lakomiaks home in Pat's car. Mike's car needed work, and Pat liked to drive anyway. It was after 11:00 when the Giangrandes stopped in at the Lakomiaks' for a nightcap.

The Lakomiaks thanked the Giangrandes for a nice time and said good-bye around midnight. By then Woody was asleep in the room he shared with his sister, Laura Diane. The violence of the afternoon had long since vanished.

Woody's problem was he had trouble getting things clean. Maybe the dishes hadn't been rinsed properly this night before they were put in the dishwasher; maybe some of the dishes hadn't been put through the washer at all. Woody said later that the dishes were too hot to take out of the dishwasher before he went to bed, and that's why the job hadn't been completed. Anyway, it hadn't been done properly, and when Pat and Michael got home Pat flew into a rage. She wanted to wake Woody up and make him do the dishes again, the right way. Michael couldn't permit it. Woody was no angel, but he didn't deserve another beating, not within hours of the last one. Woody had enough old bruises and permanent scars to mark the times he had displeased his mother. All the kids did. Michael Giangrande said no, he wouldn't allow her to get Woody out of bed.

She turned on Michael then; it was the start of a bitter oral assault that lasted about three hours. Later, the question of whether or not they'd had an "argument" would come in for a great deal of courtroom debate. There was a disagreement between husband and wife; that's certain. Michael Giangrande maintains, however, that he learned several years into his marriage that he should never argue with his wife. Arguing with her was throwing gasoline on a fire; it just aggravated her condition. A marriage counselor had told him that years before. Once, he had tape-recorded one of Pat's tirades, thinking if she heard how bad she sounded, she might try to tone it down. But the tape had no effect. Pat moved from the issue of the dishes to some larger questions. She was mad at Michael because he took sides against her, she said. He sided with the kids. He sided with all her adversaries. He sided with the neighbors in her conflagrations with them. Furiously, she recalled the time he had done this, the time he had said that. Pat's harangue continued as she walked out of the kitchen, into the living room, and into their bedroom. Laura Diane was still up, and Woody, who had been asleep, was awake by now. Woody cringed under the covers, hoping to stay out of sight and out of trouble.

Pat had a bottle of paprika oil that she'd picked up from the kitchen shelf. She wanted Michael to dump the oil into the next-door neighbor's swimming pool. When Michael refused she accused him of being a coward. Struggling with the cap, she threw the bottle at him and spilled the oil. It formed a puddle on the carpet in the bedroom. Some of the paprika oil seeped under a bandage she wore on her left hand, into a wound she'd received in an accident with a lawn mower months before.

Laura Diane got out of bed and tried to help. She got the bandaging equipment from the bathroom. Michael tried to change the bandage, but Pat wouldn't hold still. She blamed Michael and the kids for her damaged hand, for the paprika oil on the floor, and for not being able to change the bandage properly. She became hysterical and ordered Laura Diane to get her a cardboard box from the basement. She was leaving them, she said, all of them. They could fend for themselves.

Laura returned with a toilet-paper box that said "Pine Grove Motel" on the side. Pat loaded the box with her belongings and told Laura to produce another box. Laura retrieved another box from the basement. Michael watched as Pat and Laura Diane packed some more of her things. Pat took $1,000 in cash from a hiding place in the mattress of their double bed. Michael didn't know that she had hidden away that much money until she produced it, but he wasn't surprised. He reasoned later that Pat was an insecure person, particularly when it came to money. When she was ready to leave, Michael helped her put the boxes in her Chevy Nova. Woody heard the front door slam and the car drive away; then he went back to sleep.

After Pat was gone, Michael suggested that Laura Diane sleep in her parents' room. He would sleep on the couch. First, though, he had to do something about that paprika oil mess. He pulled the bed over the puddle to keep the kids from walking through it. He finally did drift off to sleep for a while, but the younger kids were up early. For about an hour, he tried painting the outside of the house, a chore he'd been meaning to get to during his vacation time, but he was exhausted and it was a hot day, and after a while he went back inside and lay down. Later he noticed the dog had gotten into the paprika oil and was tracking it all over the house. He cut out the damaged section of the carpet and replaced it with a new piece, left over from when the carpet had been installed. He and the kids made hamburgers for supper, watched some television, and went to bed.

Michael's car, also a Chevy Nova, a couple of years older than his wife's car, needed a spark plug and a new fan belt. He had purchased the replacement parts but couldn't find a ratchet that would fit the spark plug. On Saturday, Woody went down the street to see if he could borrow the right-sized ratchet from a neighbor. Woody made three trips: twice he came back with the wrong piece; the third time he came back with the neighbor. The neighbor pulled the offending spark plug out of the car. Pat had been missing for about thirty-six hours.

Mike's parents showed up to take Woody to church; he was serving the seven o'clock evening mass at St. Symphorosa's Church on Austin Avenue. They returned with him about an hour later. Mike didn't go into details with his folks, but he did say that he had had a little fight with Pat and she'd left a couple of nights ago. After his parents returned to Evergreen Park, Michael decided to go look for his wife. First he drove to the home of one of Pat's girlfriends, about two miles away. Pat had once gone to stay with this girlfriend when she and Michael had had a fight early in their marriage. Then he went by Pat's stepmother's place about eight blocks away. He went past a couple of motels. Pat had checked into a motel called the Skylark the last time she'd left, just a couple of weeks ago. He drove past the Rainbow. And the Cindy Lynn, where he and Pat used to go before they were married. Finally, he checked the Holiday Inn's parking lot, at 95th and Cicero, near his parents' apartment, for her car. He stopped and bought her a birthday card. Driving back on Cicero Avenue, he thought he saw a car that looked like his wife's, and he followed it. It was the wrong car.

● ● ●

Other than Michael Giangrande's parents, and the kids, the only person who knew about Pat's disappearance was Ed Norris. Ed's television set was broken, and he had gone to the corner tavern to watch the football game. About twenty patrons, most of whom knew who Ed was, were in the joint that night. When there was a break in the game Ed called the Giangrande house to discuss a timetable for a planned outing with his children the following day. Laura Diane told her father that Pat had taken off a couple of days earlier and Michael had gone to the racetrack. Ed Norris says he had no reason to doubt this story because he knew Michael was a heavy horseplayer. His ex-wife, after all, had met Michael at the track.

Michael Giangrande returned home at about 11:30 P.M. and ordered a pizza. NBC programs were pushed back an hour that night because of the football game, so Mike caught the end of the news and all of "Saturday Night Live." For that reason, he thought at first that it was 10:30 when he returned home. "That makes me a big liar, I guess," he would say later.

If Pat didn't return on Sunday, he promised himself, he would begin quietly making some phone calls, even though it would be humiliating to tell people that she had left him. If Pat didn't show up for her birthday, Mike would be very worried; that would be totally out of character. Also, she knew that Mike was due back at work on Monday and wouldn't be around to look after the kids. Michael slept on the couch again.

● ● ●

The night of Monday, August 27—the night he went to Kankakee to identify his wife—was the first time that Michael Giangrande told police that he hadn't seen her, or the green 1974 Chevy Nova she drove, or the two cardboard boxes since early the morning of the previous Friday. The reason the words "Pine Grove Motel" were written on the box, he explained, was that the box had first come into the house loaded with a quantity of toilet paper they had purchased from a onetime neighbor down the block who used to own the Pine Grove in the Wisconsin Dells; he was able to sell the Giangrandes toilet paper at a low price. He didn't know where Pat was headed when she took off that night, he said. Certainly not the Pine Grove Motel. Maybe, he thought, she had gone to her aunt's house in Peoria. But he had called the aunt, and she said she hadn't seen Pat. He related an abbreviated version of what happened when he and Pat returned from the Lakomiaks' that night and gave the police some of Pat's background. Suicide attempts. Child abuse conviction. Aggravated battery charge. He said his wife had been unfaithful, but he didn't know with whom. Pat had had an intrauterine device inserted some years ago by a physician in Palos Heights, he said. Michael Giangrande choked and sobbed and listed the names of her ex-husbands and doctors and told the police that there had been a problem with Laura Diane and a neighbor, no longer a friend, the year before. His wife, he said, had used other names, including Patricia Norris, Patricia Russell, Patricia Teeple, Patricia Utevice, Patricia Delgado, and Patricia Lynn. She had driver's licenses for both Patricia Giangrande and Patricia Russell. At 8:00 P.M. on Monday, the police sent out a description of Pat's car.

While her stepfather was being interviewed by one police officer, fifteen-year-old Laura Diane talked with another. She said Pat was her real mother, though they didn't get along very well and she had spent some time in a foster home. She thought her mother had taken about a thousand dollars when she left the house. Her stepfather had been home all weekend, she said at first, then later amended that to say that he left for a while Saturday night to look for her mother. Her mother had tried to kill herself a year or two ago. She said her mother had divorced her real father, Ed Norris, nine years before, and she gave them Norris's address. She said that Norris and her mother had had a fight once when Norris took Woody away, adding that her mother had been charged with aggravated battery at the time. There had been masking tape and plastic bags in her mother's car ever since June, plastic bags like the ones that were in their basement even now. Her stepfather got the plastic bags from the place where he worked, she told the policeman. Laura Diane said that her real father had a girlfriend who hated her mother.

Michael and Laura Diane left Kankakee about 8:30 that night, just before Dr. Sanders, Patricia Giangrande's dentist, arrived from Oak Brook. The dentist met with Wiseman, Jackson, Marks, and Nugent. He examined the mandible and the maxilla that Dr. Shalgos had removed from the victim's head during the autopsy the day before. Sanders identified the bones of Patricia Giangrande, on whom he had recently performed oral surgery, and left copies of x-rays and charts from her file. Mike's parents were already at his house when he got home, and together they went to the Blake-Lamb funeral home on West 63rd Street to make arrangements for a wake.

The next morning at about 11:00, Jackson and Marks drove to Evergreen Park, to the police station, to listen to the tape-recorded conversation that the police had had with Geraldine Giangrande the day before. They decided there was nothing significant on the tape, but they took it with them anyway and went to Michael's parents' home. The Giangrandes weren't there.

The elder Giangrandes had stayed overnight at Michael's house and were getting ready to go back to the funeral parlor in the afternoon and help make the final preparations for the wake that evening. They made arrangements with St. Symphorosa's for a funeral mass to be held later during the week and called a doctor to get some prescription drugs for Michael, who was still quite shaky and had not had any sleep for several days now.

The Kankakee police visited the Chicago homicide police, and together they went to the Skylark Motel to see if Pat Giangrande, or Pat Giangrande by any other name, had registered there, but she hadn't. Then they went to the Giangrande house at 60th and Parkside.

Michael and his parents had left Laura Diane in charge of the other four children and gone to the funeral home. Laura Diane called and asked Michael if it was all right if the police searched the house. Michael said sure. The police found two address books that had belonged to Pat and a photograph taken of Michael and Pat when they were married in a Catholic service a couple of months earlier at St. Symphorosa's. (They had been married in a civil ceremony at City Hall years before.) The police noted that there were a lot of clothes in the bedroom; they saw two freezers (one of them turned out to be a refrigerator), a roll of clear plastic bags, and rolls of toilet tissue in the basement. Laura explained that she had removed the toilet paper from the box she gave her mother to pack her clothes in. The police searched the garage but didn't find anything that interested them. They asked Laura Diane if her mother ever wore a glove to protect the bandage on her hand; Laura Diane said she used a turquoise rubber glove and that she would get it for the police. She looked in the bathroom, and when she didn't find the glove there, she went to the basement. But she never could find a glove.

The police asked Laura Diane about the circumstances of the past Friday morning. She said her mother was upset with her brother Woody because he hadn't done the dishes properly and she wanted to wake him. Her stepfather wouldn't let her, an argument developed, and Pat said she was leaving. Laura Diane said she helped her mother pack and carry her things to the car. Her mother left between 4:00 and 5:00 A.M., she said.

Laura Diane had no idea where her mother might have gone when she left. Her mother's foster mother, Marge Russell, lived nearby, but she didn't think her mother would go there. Her mother once had a boyfriend whose name she remembered, but she didn't remember where he lived, and she didn't think her mother would go there anyway. Her mother also had a girlfriend, but she didn't think her mother would go to her house either. Laura Diane told a strange story about her mother and her girlfriend. She said this girlfriend had a black boyfriend and that, while they were on their way to Kankakee to identify the body, her stepfather, Michael, told her that sometime during the past year her mother had been drugged by the woman and her boyfriend and forced to perform sexual perversions that they took pictures of. She said her father told her that they had used these first pictures to blackmail her mother into performing more sex acts with more black men.

She told police that her mother had taken her and the other children to the Skylark Motel a couple of weeks earlier, and they stayed in a room on the second floor. She thought maybe her mother had gone there again, or maybe she had gone to a motel she used to go to with her stepfather before they were married. Then Laura Diane told the policemen that she'd had some trouble with one of the family's southwest-side neighbors. When she told her parents the story of this neighbor and what had happened, she said, they notified the Chicago police. Laura Diane said the neighbor called and threatened to kill everyone in the family after that, because he had been reported to the police.

On Wednesday, the police received word that the green Nova had been found in the parking lot of a Venture store in Matteson, Illinois. Officers Jackson, Marks, Scroggins, and another patrolman went to the parking lot and there met the state police and Joseph Ambrozich. Ambrozich examined the car at the scene but didn't find anything. Spud Conway came with his tow truck and towed the car to his garage in Kankakee, where Ambrozich would examine it again. The police took pictures of the car and distributed them to local suburban police departments.

Jackson went to the Venture store that afternoon and talked to the employees. One employee said that he had gone to the store at about 10:00 P.M. on Sunday night to let a cleaning crew in and noticed a car parked in the lot that may have been a Chevy. A female accountant said that she saw a green Chevy Nova parked near the service station in the lot on Monday morning. According to the security chief, an electrician reported that he had been working at the service station Sunday morning and hadn't seen any car in the lot.

In the afternoon, the state police sent out three teams of investigators to canvass the southern end of the Chicago area, looking for a motel where Patricia Giangrande might have gone just prior to her death. The agents carried photos of Patricia and her car and came back with nothing. Marks and Jackson visited the Matteson police and asked them to find out if any of their officers had seen the green Chevy and if any of the local taxi drivers had picked up a fare from the store lot.

The next day, the Matteson police reported that they had checked with the cab companies to no avail. They added that the midnight patrol shift had recorded the Chevy Nova in the Venture lot on Tuesday evening. Marks and Jackson went to see Pat Giangrande's gynecologist in Palos Heights. He said she had been examined in May and that the IUD that was inserted in 1975 was still in place. Jackson showed the doctor the device that had been removed from Patricia Giangrande, and the gynecologist said it was similar to the one that had been inserted. Looking through Pat's records, the doctor said she had been treated for an injury to her fingers at the Mendota Community Hospital in June and had been admitted to Holy Cross Hospital for two days in April 1976. The doctor said he and his brother had treated her for the past nine years and she had often confided her difficulties to them.

Marks and Jackson then went to Griffith Laboratories in Alsip, Illinois, where Michael Giangrande worked. The personnel manager told them that Michael had been a batcher there for several years. The personnel director told them that he was hardworking, dependable, very prompt, and worked a lot of overtime. Mr. Giangrande needed the work, he said, because he had a large family. The police asked if Michael would have access to clear plastic bags and masking tape, and the personnel manager said he would. They talked to a couple of other bosses at the plant and asked if Michael used any knives or saws in his work, and they were told that he didn't. They asked if there was any way he could have gotten into the plant after working hours, and the personnel director said that they employed a security firm and it would not have been possible for anyone to get into the plant after working hours.

The day before their mother's funeral, Ed Norris took Laura Diane and Woody to lunch. Ed remarked that the photograph displayed on top of the closed casket was a flattering likeness, a very professional job. Ed thought the two teenagers had remarkably little to say about their dead mother. In conversation, Laura Diane told Ed that the police had asked where Michael was on Saturday night. She said she had reported to them that he was in the house all night. They were all so worried about Pat, Laura Diane said, that they had been unable to sleep; therefore, Michael could not have left home without her knowledge. "I said, 'Well, Laura Diane, when I called up over there Saturday night and he wasn't home, you told me he was at the racetrack,' " Ed Norris said. Reminded of this story, Ed added, Laura Diane's mouth dropped open.

On Friday, there was a funeral at St. Symphorosa's for Patricia Giangrande. After the mass, the family and a few friends and the people from the Blake-Lamb Funeral Home drove down to Peoria, where Patricia was buried in a plot next to her father. The elder Giangrandes took home Michael, who was still heavily sedated, and then for the first time in five days they went back to their own apartment in Evergreen Park. Geraldine Giangrande slept for hours.

• • •

You might say that Patricia Giangrande was a troubled woman. And that might have been the worst thing anybody ever said about her had she died in a more conventional way. As it is, she's been called many things by many people, most of whom she never met. One of the members of the team that prosecuted the case said, "She was a piece of dirt. Trash." Paul Bradley, Michael Giangrande's attorney, said, "The woman could have pissed off Christ in ten seconds." Bradley had heard the tape Mike made of Pat shrieking at the kids.

Patricia Giangrande was thrown away as a child. She was born Eugenia Delgado Teeple in Peoria, to an alcoholic father and a mother who abandoned her when she was six months old. The Russells, a middle-aged couple her father knew, lived in Chicago. They agreed to take care of her as long as her father sent money for room and board. Her father never did send much to support her. But the Russells, who had already raised a foster son, took care of the little girl anyway.

When Pat was an adult she told people that she had been mistreated by the Russells, even though there was no reason to believe this story.

Over the years, she often returned to her foster parents' house. She grew close to her father's sister, Jean, who also lived in Peoria, and she sporadically saw her father. When she ran into him she usually tried to get money from him. Michael Giangrande thought that Pat's pattern of taking money from men in return for affection was established by her early experience with her father. Pat was with the

Russells until she reached age sixteen and married Richard Lynn of Peoria. Even then she habitually ran away, from her foster family's home on the south side, from her blood relations, and from her husband. Kathy Lee Lynn was born when Pat was nineteen years old. Kathy Lee's father left the picture almost as quickly as Pat's mother had abandoned her. A couple of years later, Pat was again living with her stepmother, Marge Russell, when she met Ed Norris. Norris was about five years older, but he had never been married, and he lived with his parents in a nice middle-class area of Chicago at 88th and Wood. Pat and Ed were married in 1963, and the family—including Kathy Lynn—moved to an apartment at 63rd and Spaulding. The baby was just two years old when her mother beat her over the head with a pipe. Kathy Lee was hospitalized, criminal charges were brought against Pat, and the child was removed from the Norris home—but not very far removed, as it turned out. Custody of Kathy Lee was awarded to Marge Russell, so Kathy was raised by her foster grandmother, the same way her mother had been raised. The Norrises' first child, Laura Diane, was born on September 7, 1965, one of few significant dates in his life that Ed Norris remembered distinctly.

During her stormy eight-year second marriage, Pat Norris had a history of mental illness and infrequent employment. She worked in a box factory, a packaging plant, and a number of south side cocktail lounges. "She never really worked anywhere for any length of time," Ed Norris recalled. Pat would hold a job at one place for a couple of months and get fired, then she would go to another place for a while and get fired, then she would go back to the first place. "Money or the things it would buy seemed to be her main objective in life," according to Ed Norris. But her craziness hampered her ability to earn a steady income. "She would go into these irrational fits of raving about something, anything, either real or imagined," Norris explained. "She had a hell of a complex; she felt everyone was trying to do something to her and was against her. She was very, very paranoid. The least little thing would set her off. Especially with the kids, the littlest thing would make her into a screaming maniac."

During the seven years they lived together, Norris said, he was working two jobs and did not sleep more than two or three hours a night. "When I was home the battle raged on. It stopped long enough for me to go to work and then started when I came home. You almost developed a sympathy for her: this poor little kid who had been picked on all her life by everybody. You felt sorry for her. Like when she used to fight with the neighbors, I felt sorry for her. But when you keep having to move, you begin to think that every neighbor can't be wrong. It can't be everybody else all the time. It's got to be her."

But the Norrises were moving up in the world as well as around in it. They lived in several south side apartments before they scraped together enough money to buy a relatively new brick house in the older section of suburban Oak Forest. "It was a picture-book-type thing," Norris said. "We had the house with this huge lot and a little stream running through the back." At Pat's insistence the Norrises were married in the Catholic Church. Another child, a son several years younger than Laura Diane, had been born. Adrian came along while they were living in Oak Forest.

The family was stigmatized by Pat Norris's sickness, however. After she attacked Kathy Lee Lynn she was in and out of the psychiatric unit at Hines Hospital in Chicago. During her marriage to Ed Norris, she tried to kill herself a couple of times. The attempt he remembered most vividly had been, he thought, rather feeble. "She ate a whole bottle of tranquillizers one of the psychiatrists had prescribed for her, and she must have done it shortly before I came inside the house. When I found her and the suicide note I took her into the bathroom and made her vomit. The pills were still whole. She must have taken them when she heard my car pull up in front of the house."

It was 1967, Norris recalled, when Pat decided to find her real mother. She located the woman in Ludington, Michigan, and visited her. Her mother was not particularly overjoyed to see her, and, Ed thought, this may have contributed to her mental condition. "She went to all these psychiatrists," he said. "I even took her to a private psychiatrist for a time. But I just couldn't financially continue it. It cost $35 an hour, and he wanted to see her three times a week. The doctor felt it would take at least two years to get to the root of her problem. He thought it all stemmed from her childhood, which it probably did."

Whatever the reason, she was always harder on the children than on herself. One day Ed Norris got a phone call at work. Laura Diane and Woody were in the hospital, and Pat was in jail for beating them. The baby was all right; she had been left with a neighbor. For a short time after that Pat was treated at the Tinley Park Mental Health

Center, a large state facility in a south suburb near Oak Forest. Woody and Laura Diane were placed in a foster home across town in the northwest suburb of Arlington Heights; only Adrian was left at home. The house in Oak Forest had to be sold to pay Pat's legal bills.

The Norrises had entered into a period of separating and reuniting that would last for several years. "It's very obvious in retrospect—I have twenty-twenty hindsight—that the first time we separated we should have gotten a divorce and gotten it over with. Society dictates to us that we're supposed to be married and we should really strive to make it work no matter how difficult it is. Pat had already been divorced once, and I don't think she wanted to get divorced again. Nor did I. So we continued this fighting, separating, and going back together. When we were separated I didn't follow her around to see what she was doing and who she was spending time with. She was one of the biggest liars I ever met in my life," Ed said. "She lied just to be lying. I never encountered anybody like that. I can see somebody lying to save face or to cover up, but she lied just in general conversation." So, even if she had told him where she had been or what she had been doing, he would not have believed her.

Despite the deception, Ed Norris must have been aware of the fact that Pat was often with Michael Giangrande. During their final separation in 1969, while Pat was living in an apartment on 63rd and Maplewood, Lisa was born. Though Pat had four children—Laura Diane, Woody, Adrian, and Lisa—while legally married to Ed Norris, Michael has always maintained that he fathered Adrian and Lisa. He even filed a paternity suit that was, for reasons that are unclear, later dropped. Norris claimed that all four children belong to him.

• • •

Michael Giangrande was born almost forty years ago on the near west side, in the Italian neighborhood where both Geraldine and Vito Giangrande had grown up. He was baptized at the Santa Maria Addolorata Church, adjacent to where they lived near Ada and Ohio. Both Mike and his sister, Marge, who was two years older, attended the parochial school attached to the church. Michael's life was fairly ordinary until he got sick.

There was a movie marathon, a six-feature film festival held at a neighborhood theater the same day that Mike's mother was having a bunch of the relatives over for a family reunion. Michael, who was eight years old, thought he would much rather see some movies than sit with the family all day. The party was so hectic that at first the family didn't notice that Mike had been gone from home an inordinately long time. "It wasn't dangerous then. It wasn't like it is now," Geraldine Giangrande said. "You didn't really start to worry until after it had already gotten dark." Geraldine told Vito he'd better go out and look for Michael.

Michael was sitting in the back of the darkened theater, where he had been sitting all day. His legs ached so badly he couldn't move. Finally, an usher noticed him crying. Michael said he couldn't walk. The usher spoke to the manager of the theater, and, when he closed the place, the manager carried Michael to his car and drove him home. When Mike's mother answered the door the manager was standing there with Michael in his arms. The next day, when the pain didn't subside, his parents called the family doctor, who examined Michael and told the Giangrandes to keep him in bed and watch carefully for any signs of a change in his condition. His parents checked every day for the next three days. There was no change. On Thursday, his ankles began to swell. His father carried him back to the doctor's office. The swelling was what the doctor had been waiting for, and now he was certain that Michael had rheumatic fever; he rushed the boy into the hospital. Michael was supervised closely and given penicillin treatments for eight days. After that the doctor sent him home, but he didn't walk for nine months. His parents carried him everywhere, and he got very thin. Most days his mother made him a malt or a milkshake to try to bring his weight up. Even after the worst part of the fever was over he couldn't roughhouse with the other kids. The Giangrandes got rid of his scooters and bicycles. He watched television and listened to the radio. Sometimes he would watch his friends play baseball. When he returned to school he was a year behind his classmates.

Michael Giangrande was about ten years old when he was hospitalized for appendicitis. The doctor ordered ice packs and a rubber sheet in an effort to bring down the fever long enough to operate. Michael was on the table when the appendix ruptured and burst. Gangrene kept him in the hospital for two months. By the time he was well again he was way behind in school, so he was enrolled in a CYO program and his mother took him downtown two or three days a week after school for remedial reading classes. His only outside activities after that were duties as an altar boy and a patrol boy.

"Michael knew the situation," his mother said. "He knew he couldn't run around and play strenuous games." Geraldine Giangrande said she became very close to Mike because he was such a sickly child.

Once out of grammar school, he was never seriously ill again. Remarkably, the rheumatic fever had no lasting effect on his heart. Mike attended Holy Trinity High School for about a year, but he was older than the other kids; his father, who worked construction, was out of a job; and now there was a five-year-old brother, Mark, to worry about. He quit school after that first year and went to work lugging beef at a warehouse on Fulton Street in the market district. In 1955, he was putting in about seventy-five hours a week and bringing home $200. When he did have time to socialize he went over to a storefront clubhouse loosely affiliated with the church and the CYO; the club's name, the Diablos, had been changed shortly after its formation to the Crusaders. Michael played basketball with the Crusaders. His best friend at the time was a guy named Tony, and together they played a lot of pinochle and hung around the neighborhood candy store, where Mike had a charge account. Mike said his next job was at American Color Type, where he mixed ink for the presses; that lasted about a year. He was about seventeen when he went to work at the A&P meat warehouse on 42nd and Kildare, cleaning up at night and on weekends. Less than a year went by before Michael and a buddy decided on a whim to volunteer for the draft. They both figured they were going to end up in Korea anyway. Geraldine Giangrande wasn't too crazy about the idea, for a couple of reasons. Vito's brother, a Marine, had recently been killed there, for one. Michael trained for four months at Fort Leonard Wood, Missouri, before he was shipped overseas. He spent fourteen months cooking at an army camp in Korea, seven miles from the action; he rarely left the base. He said his tour of duty was longer than it was supposed to be because the army was short of cooks at the time. He came home for thirty days, then was sent to Fort Carson in Colorado Springs, where he finished his hitch doing field maneuvers. When he was discharged he went back to live with his parents, who were by now living farther west on Saint Louis Avenue, in the same building with his sister Marge and her husband and former high school sweetheart, Vince Aparo. Michael returned to the A&P and worked cleanup at the warehouse for another three years.

Michael Giangrande was terribly shy around girls. When he got out of the service Vince remembers trying to fix him up by inviting him and an eligible girl over to Sunday dinner. Predictably, though, that never worked out, and Vince and Marge gave up after a while. When he was twenty years old Mike clipped a coupon from the paper and enrolled in a Fred Astaire dance class at the downtown studio, which at the time was located near State and Randolph. "You would go there three times a week," Michael said. "The first week was evaluation and tests; after that you learned a step a week. The box step. The fox trot. The samba. The cha-cha." The Fred Astaire people told him he was great, and he signed up for $3,000 worth of lessons. "You know," he said, "$25 a week for the rest of your life."

Of course, there was a dance instructor, a nice little girl with long, red hair and a thirty-eight-inch bust. One day Mike came in for his lesson and his regular instructor wasn't there, so he danced with the redhead. He started coming to the studio during the daytime so he could dance with her. She wasn't allowed to go out with the customers, but Michael finally convinced her to take a walk with him in Grant Park after work. For a couple of weeks they walked through the park together. They talked and talked. They necked. The Fred Astaire studio sponsored a moonlight dance, a kind of graduation party, and they walked to the Crusaders' storefront after the dance. It was late at night, and there was nobody there. "I thought, 'Great, she's going to do it,' " Mike said. "And I finally get her clothes off, and she starts crying—so I told her to get dressed. We never saw each other after that. What I should've done was made love to her, I guess."

For the next four or five years he lugged beef off a truck at the A&P on the day shift, then worked cleanup at night, when the money was better. He took the government test to become a meat inspector twice, but the job involved a transfer out of town and he didn't want to leave. Most of the time he lived at home, though once in a while a deal came up where he would move in with a buddy for a while. He had a friend named Ziggy who lived in Wisconsin and did some work for the Canteen Corporation in Chicago. Ziggy and Mike took an apartment in Lawndale. That didn't last long.

Mike had little use for an apartment anyway. Sometimes he would take a girl out to dinner and a show at the Oriental or the State-Lake, but it never amounted to much. "One girl I took out . . . we parked my Oldsmobile at Grand Avenue and Lake Shore Drive. We're necking, and I thought I heard her say, 'Push the seat back.' So I'm playing around with the seat, and she says, 'What are you doing?' and I tell her I'm pushing the seat back, and she says, 'I didn't say, "Push the seat back"; I said, "The police are in back of us." ' And I turned around, and there they were. That was really funny. There's really nobody else that I'd like to mention. . . . There were a lot of horny women around the A&P and around the neighborhood."

He applied for a job as a meat cutter and spent three years boning briskets before he returned to the job as meat lugger. When that got slow he went back on nights as a selector, filling orders for stores. If a store wanted ten boxes of hot dogs, he'd fill ten boxes with hot dogs. He was almost thirty, and working with meat in thirty-two- to thirty-six-degree temperatures was giving him bursitis trouble in his shoulders.

There was this cab driver named Tommy who used to hang out at Washington Park. He was always playing the horses, and he was always up to his neck in juice. He would rent a cab and take it out of the garage, but he almost never made his nut. Everybody has his own Tommy, the friend in need, the guy you see only when he wants to borrow money or needs some kind of favor. Tommy was, of course, an albatross and a parasite, but he was Michael Giangrande's parasite, attached to Michael the way Angel Martin was attached to Jim Rockford. Michael never got anything from Tommy except a pain in the neck and some amusement. But Michael kept him around and was even saddened when he heard one day that Tommy had keeled over and died of a heart attack while waiting in the cab line for a fare at the airport. Anyway, Tommy had this pattern. He would go to the track, blow all his money, then go down to the bus station and pick up some people from out of town who looked dumb; he'd drive them up and down the expressway for four or five hours, take them where they were going, and make enough money to break even for the night.

One summer afternoon, Mike said, Tommy called him at work and asked him if he wanted to go to the track that night. Michael agreed, and Tommy came by after Michael had finished his shift at A&P. "We can't go straight out there," Tommy told Mike as soon as he got into the cab. "I've got to pick up this girl I met at the bus station last night. She's supposed to be waiting at 63rd Street." Mike thought this was peculiar because Tommy had never shown any interest in women. As it came to light, Tommy did not have a standard date in mind. He wanted to trade the girl to some guy he knew at the track to settle an old debt. They picked up the woman and headed out to the park.

Michael Giangrande got lucky that night. He started winning right away, and by the third race he was collecting $75–$80 a race. The girl was more than willing to cash in his tickets and place his bets for him. They had been there about an hour when he and the girl started necking between the races. Then during the races. They forgot all about Tommy. By the time the track closed, Michael had the girl and a couple hundred dollars. It was time for Tommy to take her back to the barn area, for the trade. Michael refused to let her go. "Those guys are gonna kill me," Tommy said ruefully, but he gave Mike and the girl a ride to a motel where they made love all night. According to Mike, they made love every day for the next three weeks. Over that three-week period, Patricia Norris's story emerged, and it was a weird story right from the start.

• • •

Around the time the Norrises moved to Oak Forest, before Adrian was born, the family went on a camping trip to Wisconsin. Ed, Pat, Ed's parents, and the two kids were in the car a short distance from the campground. Pat flew into a rage. "The weather had been lousy, and everybody was on edge because of that," Ed said. "Something set her off—I don't know what it was—and she decided she was going back to Chicago. I begged her. I pleaded with her. I did everything short of throwing her bodily back into the car. She knew where we were camping, so I figured I'd let her get out of the car. Eventually she would just walk back there. But she didn't. She got back to Chicago some way or other. Maybe she hitchhiked. I don't know how she got back, but she got back." At this point, Ed Norris's account of the incident contradicts Michael Giangrande's story. According to Michael, Pat told him that she hitchhiked south a way and got somebody to give her bus fare. She met Tommy at the bus station, he loaned her some money, and they went to the track together, where they blew everything they had. Norris claimed that Pat was in the house when he arrived home with the children the next day.

Mike said that during the next month Pat lived with her stepmother and saw him frequently. She disappeared and turned up again. Mike never asked any questions. She disappeared and turned up again, this time looking for a handout. Every so often she would arrive on his doorstep, stay a few days, and ask for $50. He knew she had three or four other guys on the line for the same kind of deal. Then she disappeared for some months. One night she arranged to meet Michael at a restaurant; she barely had enough money to eat, and she said she was living with her stepmother again. Her husband was back in town, but he'd pawned the kids off on some woman. Pat told Mike she needed $500 for a lawyer. She'd beat up on one of the kids, and they were taking her to court. Mike had only $200, but he gave it to her anyway. She was also pregnant with her fourth child at the time, a child Mike is convinced is his. She obtained some more money from some other guy and disappeared again. She came back and lived with Michael for a while. (He had his own apartment by now, expressly for such a purpose.) She told Michael that she and Ed Norris were divorced. She disappeared again. She tried to commit suicide by taking an overdose. She disappeared again. She said that she'd remarried Norris. She had another baby girl.

A few days after Christmas, 1969, Mike received a call from Pat's stepmother, who asked him to go to the Norris home in Oak Forest because she thought something bad was happening there. Something bad *was* happening there. "It was somewhere around the holidays," Ed Norris said. "The ex-wife had supposedly gone to visit her mother in Michigan for a few days. I found out she wasn't with her mother; she was with Giangrande." Ed had made up his mind that he wasn't going to argue about it. He managed to stay calm until Pat began unpacking her suitcase. "I had bought her a red negligee for Christmas. When I saw that red negligee come out of the suitcase, it was like waving a red flag in front of a bull. I bought her this red negligee for Christmas, and she was wearing it with somebody else. I was so upset. . . ." Norris admitted that he slapped her around.

Michael was on his way to the rescue. "I asked this part-time guy from work to go out there with me for protection. I knocked on the door, and Pat answered. Both of her eyes are black and blue. Some of her teeth were missing. Her hair'd been ripped out of her head, and she was bare-ass naked. Norris is in the next room, he's naked too, and Adrian's in her crib screamin' her lungs out."

Ed Norris said he was asleep by the time Mike Giangrande and his friend arrived. Neither husband disputed the fact that Mike and his friend, in Mike's words, "beat the hell" out of Ed Norris. Michael took the baby to his mother's and took Pat to a restaurant, to a doctor, and finally home to his apartment. The next day Pat's stepmother took snapshots of her bruises in case she needed them when she filed for divorce. Norris said he never even thought about contesting it. "You wouldn't believe how glad I was to get away from that situation," Ed said later. "Generally speaking, when there's a divorce you split up property or something. But I got nothing but the clothes on my back. She got the house, the car, the furniture, the kids. I got nothing. I didn't want anything. I just wanted to get away from her."

While she was waiting for her divorce to come through, Pat had another baby, Lisa. The divorce was final on the 17th of November, 1970, and Pat and Mike were married two days later. They moved into the duplex at 6409 S. Long that she got in the divorce settlement. Michael stopped going to the track, started working twelve hours a day and saving money. He was a stable influence. Soon after they were married, Pat and Michael Giangrande got custody of Laura Diane and Woody.

● ● ●

Michael Giangrande said that he first found out his wife was mentally ill when they went to retrieve Laura Diane and Woody from the foster family they were living with in Arlington Heights. It was a rotten winter day. There was a lot of snow around. Michael and Pat had driven in Pat's '67 Chevy Caprice to pick up a panel truck in a western suburb. Michael was supposed to drive the truck, which they needed to move the kids' belongings in, and Pat would follow behind him in the car. Michael pulled out of the parking lot, and Pat backed up to pull out behind him, but she backed into a boulder, hidden by the snow, and became hopelessly stuck. There was a car behind Michael's that looked like the Caprice—it was getting dark—and Mike was satisfied that she was driving behind him. Michael waited for her at the foster parents' home, and she finally showed up in a cab. The family piled into the panel truck, and Pat began screaming at the kids. She said it was their fault that the car was stuck in the parking lot and that they had to go back for it. It was also their fault—Laura Diane, who was about eight years old, and Woody, who was six—that the cab ride cost her $18. It was their fault for putting Mike through all this. She cursed and swore. "That was the first time I ever saw her in that kind of mood," Michael said. By the time they got back to the parking lot, the police had towed the car away.

Mike's brother-in-law Vince drove him to the pound the next day to get the car back. The car wouldn't start, so they paid a mechanic who had a garage across the street to tow it again and fix it. The mechanic put in a new starter, but the car still wouldn't work. Finally they figured out that the spark-plug wires had been switched so the engine wouldn't fire, to eliminate the danger of somebody's taking the car from the pound without paying the towing fee. Michael spent most of the day trying to get the car back, paying the police $50 and the mechanic across the street $45. He resolved not to tell his wife about any of it; it was his first alliance with her children.

During his last few years at A&P, Mike was working maintenance or whatever job gave him the most hours at the best pay. The grocery chain was phasing out its meat packaging by the early '70s, and almost everything that came into the place was prepackaged. Mike was a selector again for a time, then went back to cleanup. As the processing operation was closed, some of the employees were allowed to take tools that were too old or too useless to be resold. Michael got a couple of knives and some rusty meat hooks, which he took home.

For a year or so after their marriage, Pat and Mike lived in the duplex she had bought with Ed Norris at 64th and Long. They hated it there and spent much of their free time looking for a bigger and better house. They found a place that they fell in love with at 6040 S. Parkside, just half a block west of the chain-link fence that outlines Midway Airport. The houses on Parkside are mostly three-bedroom bungalows made of light-colored brick with picture windows in the center, which give them the look of large blank faces staring across the street at each other. Small front yards and backyards and two-car garages surround each house, and there are perhaps ten feet separating the buildings from one another on each side. Neighbors cannot be anonymous in such close quarters, and many build high fences in an effort to maintain privacy in their own backyards. The Giangrandes put the duplex on Long Street up for sale. But they couldn't find a buyer. Rather than get stuck with two mortgages, they deeded the place—which was six blocks away from the new house—to Ed Norris, and he moved back in.

Both Michael Giangrande and his brother-in-law Vince got laid off from their jobs at A&P in 1975. The warehouse closed entirely for a while. Mike was unable to find another job, and Pat was about to have another baby. Mike went on unemployment and collected $135 a week. He learned that the Veterans Administration would pay him

$440 a month to go to school, so he enrolled in hairdressing school. The A&P reopened with a skeleton crew, but Mike was not taken back. Neither was Vince. When the VA money ran out, he went to Add-A-Man, a day labor outfit on the south side. Mike said he would sometimes get to Add-A-Man around 5:00 A.M., work an eight-hour shift at the Clorox plant, then shoot back to Add-A-Man for another eight-hour assignment at the Kool-Aid factory. By working sixteen hours a day at $2.40 an hour, he could take home about $36. He worked at Add-A-Man using the name Pat Norris and his wife's Social Security number so he could continue to collect unemployment under his own name.

One day Add-A-Man sent him to Griffith Laboratories in Alsip. At the end of the shift the foreman asked if he could come back the next day. Mike explained that he had been sent out by a temporary agency and would have to ask their permission. Add-A-Man agreed, and Mike worked for time-and-a-half on Saturday and Sunday. The foreman told him to stop by personnel on Monday, and Griffith would give him a regular, full-time job. Mike explained about his working and collecting and signed up at Griffith using his real name and Social Security number. He was hired as a spice mixer at $4 an hour. His first day he worked from 7:00 A.M. until 10:30 or 11 that night, earning about five hours of overtime. The foreman told him that he did a nice job and could work as many hours as he wanted. Right from the outset he was putting in eighty-five to ninety-five hours a week. His first year, at the $4 rate, he brought home about $20,000. He got some twenty-five-cent raises along the way and the next year made about $26,000. Michael Giangrande was making the most money he ever made—sometimes as much as $625 a week.

Michael ran a 10,000-pound mixer in which he would put together mixes for soups, pizza seasonings, fish batters, and coatings for chicken and beef. He was not allowed to divulge the secret recipes, some of which were sold to fast-food chains like Jericho, which operates the Long John Silver's restaurants, among others. It was a rough job just in terms of the weights he was dealing with, and the fifteen- to eighteen-hour days precluded any social life, though that didn't bother him much. He was still very quiet. He bowled with the league at work. He missed going to the track once in a while, but he had never been much of a track or a bar person. Pat was the one who knew all the people and liked to drink. (Ed Norris said that he never saw a friendly side, if his ex-wife had one. "She wasn't a very likable person," he said. "In fact, when she disappeared there were theories that she had stayed at some girlfriend's house or something like that. To be blunt about it, she didn't have any friends, so staying at anybody's house was out of the question as far as I know. Unless she had developed a friend somewhere that nobody knew about.")

Acquaintances substantiate what Mike says about himself: he would just as soon be at work as socialize. Anyhow, he was feeding five kids and supporting a wife with wild spending habits. Michael Giangrande needed the money.

● ● ●

The marriage was erratic. Mike first learned about Pat's infidelity sometime in 1971, he said, when they both worked at A&P. Mike was on the day shift, and Pat was working nights. "One night she never came home until 3:00 A.M." Mike said she cried and told him about being in a man's bedroom while he had another woman waiting in the closet. "After that I made a pact with her: if that's what she was going to do, do it and be discreet about it."

Though Ed Norris emphatically denied Mike Giangrande's charge that he and Pat continued to have a sexual relationship after their divorce and Pat's marriage to Mike, he admitted the common bond of the children and proximity kept them in touch. Even while they were going through the divorce, Ed said, Pat would stop by to show him dime-store items—like a tube of lipstick—she had shoplifted. "I guess it was hard for her to break old habits," Norris said. "The only friends we had in our marriage were people who were my friends prior to our marriage, and little by little she had gotten rid of all of them. So when we were married and while we were married I was her husband, I was her friend, I was her confidante. I was her only contact with the outside world. After she was remarried it was the same way. The only difference was she had a husband. I was still a friend. She would call me up and tell me all her problems. Every once in a while she would stop over here to discuss things with me. Sometimes she'd bring the kids with her. Sometimes she'd come by herself. I could communicate with her much better after we were divorced than I ever did when we were married."

Mike Giangrande said he put up with sexual indiscretions and her relationship, whatever it was, with Ed Norris because he was sympathetic to her mental problems. Pat had never taken any great pains to hide her history of mental illness. Michael knew that the years 1969 and 1970 were particularly traumatic. Besides the fact that her marriage to Ed Norris was a shambles, her natural mother, tired of Pat's impromptu visits, told her she never wanted to see her again. Mike said Pat told him her mother had said, "I left you when you were three years old, and I don't want you coming around here now." Mike knew she attempted suicide after she returned from that visit and had ended up in Hines Hospital for a couple of weeks. When she got out she told people it was just a vacation, a rest, she had a ball playing games with all the crazy people. It seemed to Mike that his wife always had pills around, and, even though she saw psychiatrists, he thought there were too many different kinds of drugs for them all to be prescribed for her. "She had Quaaludes and Seconals, 'blues,' some kind of heroin derivative, nerve pills, and tranquilizers. She had a dresser draw just loaded with pills." Pat took an overdose once while they were married, went into convulsions, and was hospitalized at Holy Cross. Michael wasn't sure whether the overdose was intended or accidental.

Oddly enough, Ed Norris remembered more about this third suicide attempt than he does about the previous two. It was a Sunday, and Ed had taken the two older children for a visit. They returned to find the Giangrande house empty; the younger kids were with the woman next door. The neighbor explained that Mike had taken Pat to the hospital. The irony of the situation, according to Norris, was that the paramedics had removed Pat's false teeth while trying to revive her. While the Giangrandes were at the hospital, the dog ate her false teeth. "When she woke up that really set her off," Norris said.

(Ed Norris and Mike Giangrande agreed that Pat was very meticulous about her appearance and obsessive in regard to her teeth. When the Norrises were married they had visited Ed's brother-in-law, who had a place west of town, in Aurora on the Fox River. On Friday night a tooth fell out of Pat's upper plate. She walked around with her hand over her mouth until Saturday morning, when she located a dentist who would repair the damage. The dentist did not do a very good job, however, and the tooth fell out again several hours later. The Norrises had to leave immediately for Chicago, Pat insisted; she could not stay there with a missing tooth.)

Despite their "pact," Michael caught his wife in other sexually compromising situations a couple of times. Once she came home from her job as a cocktail waitress, and Mike found a rubber left in her vagina by a previous occupant. Then there was the insurance man who visited their home about four times a week. "My wife was the kind of person who didn't get dressed until two o'clock in the afternoon. I was gone at seven or eight in the morning. And this guy would come over. . . . The only reason I found out about it was that she wanted to end it. He was supposed to have been paying the insurance premiums for her; come to find out we get a letter that the premiums haven't been paid for six months. Turns out the guy's been doing this with a lot of clients, and he gets fired." The insurance agent beat Pat Giangrande at her own game. Michael thought there were quite a few occasions when she said she was going to see her girlfriend but really went someplace else. After a while, she didn't bother to call him with an excuse. "It was funny in a way . . . black humor . . . she always thought she was doing these things to me. She was really doing things to herself."

Pat Giangrande confided to Ed Norris that Mike had accused her of having an affair with the insurance agent. Supposedly, Pat implied that Mike was imagining liaisons out of insane jealousy. According to Norris, Pat was very indignant about Mike's false accusations. She reported that Mike had made the outrageous charge that she was carrying on with a clergyman. But Pat also told Ed Norris that Mike was gone from the house so much and was so tired when he came home that their sex life had suffered.

●　●　●

The violence got worse. Michael woke up one morning and found her standing over the bed holding a knife. She told him she was going to kill him. "She was taking a lot of Seconals then. I ended up talking her out of it." More often the violence involved the kids somehow, and Michael had more trouble dealing with that. If the kids didn't get hurt by their mother when she was in a rage, they always got scared.

The week before Labor Day, 1977, Mike said, Woody disappeared. Pat called Ed Norris to ask if he had seen Woody, and he said that he hadn't. The Giangrandes thought that Norris was lying and tried to enlist the help of the police to get Woody back. But the police said they couldn't do much in light of the fact that Norris was Woody's natural father.

Pat found out that Ed was taking Woody to a Parents without Partners picnic in Schiller Park, so she and Mike went out to the picnic grounds. They found Norris and then Woody. Pat grabbed Woody and put him in the Giangrandes' car. That wasn't enough. She took a knife from her purse and stabbed Norris in the back. There was a fight, Norris was stabbed several more times, and Pat was cut on the hand. She was taken away by the police and charged with aggravated battery. Norris went to the hospital to get sewn up. Woody took off, and Mike went after him. "She told police she stabbed Norris because he took the kid and he hadn't been paying any child support. But I think she really wanted revenge. She couldn't accept the fact that he had the nerve to take Woody away from her."

Ed Norris told a slightly different version of the story: Pat had thrown Woody out of the house, so he had gone to stay with Ed. The picnic was planned, Ed was going, and he saw no reason not to bring Woody along. "I only caught a glimpse of her," Norris said. "She came up behind me, and I thought it was somebody I hadn't seen in a long time slapping me on the back. She stabbed me twice in the back, and as I turned she got me twice in the chest. She was screaming something. The only clear word was *son-of-a-bitch*. Then she just ran away. I didn't see Michael, but I understand he drove her over there. She was too nervous or too upset to drive herself. I don't think Giangrande knew what she was up to." The Giangrandes subsequently got back Woody and the car, which had been impounded by the police. Ed Norris dropped the charges. Michael said his wife threatened to kill Ed if he didn't.

Ed Norris, who admitted that he was not paying child support at the time, said that pursuing the charges against Pat was more trouble than it was worth. "I got tired of taking time off work to go to court. I had already gone about fourteen different times, and I knew what the outcome was going to be. She would get probation and would have to go see a psychiatrist for the next two or three years."

●　●　●

In the beginning, Mike would react. He would argue. He would let it get to him. But, he said, when he fought back he only created more trouble. Pat was diagnosed as a manic-depressive, he says; without any warning she would become angry or jumpy. Vince said he had trouble being around her—getting physically close—because she was so hyperactive and nervous. There was a period when Pat was in therapy at a city mental health center on Pulaski. Her doctor called

Mike and asked him if he would come and join group therapy. The doctor, he reported, ended up advising him not to fight back. "She wanted instant answers. She wouldn't tell anybody anything. If you have problems you've got to talk. I stopped going because it was a waste of time." But he followed the advice. Michael Giangrande said that for the last five years of their marriage they never had a real fight. "If she said black was white, I said OK." Sometimes his passivity got him into trouble, like the time he tried to steal a carton of cigarettes from the K-Mart because she had demanded the cigarettes but thrown him out of the house without any money. He was arrested for shoplifting.

Mike feared that his refusal to react may have made life worse for the kids. After a while, Pat started leaving. "She'd leave for a week; sometimes she'd take the kids and sometimes she wouldn't. She'd say she was going to Michigan or Peoria. I'd say to her, 'What the hell are you going to do in Michigan or Peoria?'

"Besides screwin' the insurance man in front of them . . . I've got a thirteen-year-old son [Woody] who must have seen every inch of my wife's body; she never wore any underwear. Of course, I got on her case about it, but she was lazy, I don't know. . . . My wife never did any housework. The kids did the wash, dried the clothes in the dryer, or hung it on the lines. She never cooked. The kids cooked or I cooked. I would do the floors. She never dusted. They lost a lot of their childhood. . . . I wanted to send the kids to college. I said I wouldn't force them to go, but it's the best thing you can do for yourself. Bartenders marry drunks. Educated people marry other educated people. . . . My wife was a schemer. She was always remodeling the house. She had me working all the time. She stayed up nights, and she added and she figured. If I could work this much, then we could put that much in the bank. She had invested in certificates. She scheduled how much she'd need until I was fifty-nine years old. We were going to be on easy street, she'd say. We were going to have at least $60,000 in the bank. . . . Despite all the things she did, I was madly in love with my wife. Blame it all on me. It's all my fault. She kept breaking up with her husband and coming back to me, and I would let her do it."

• • •

Pat Giangrande's father lived with the family for a couple of months before he died in April 1979 of cancer of the throat. Michael explained that he just showed up on their doorstep one day. "When you get old you seek out your children," Mike explained. He was in his late seventies, an intelligent man ruined by alcohol. Some nights, Mike would sit up and talk to him. At the end he was bedridden, in Pat and Mike's bed, and hemorrhaged for days. They buried him in Peoria. In a peculiar way, Pat had been close to her father, even though they were often separated. She took his death very hard.

Then, in June, there was the accident with her hand. In 1977, the Giangrandes had looked at a plot of land in the Woodhaven development, about three hours from Chicago, within a couple of hours of the Iowa border. Woodhaven is a luxurious campground. There are sports facilities, "common areas," a lake, and a security force. People buy small parcels of land (60 by 100 feet) where they can keep trailers and campers. Camping had never been one of the "great joys" of his life, Michael said, but after a while Pat just had to have the property. The real estate agent stayed on the case after they returned to Chicago to think it over, and finally, in 1978, Michael relented and they bought the property, financing it through the Harris Bank. The first thing that they had to do, before they could buy a camper, was to clear the land. The weeds had grown nearly waist deep during the time the agent was trying to close the deal. When the weather began to get warm in the spring of 1979, the Giangrandes went to Woodhaven to weed. They took lawnmowers, gardening tools, and large plastic bags that Mike got from work to dispose of the weeds. They had cleared about a third of the plot when something got stuck in the lawnmower. Pat kept trying to pull it out. "I must have told her forty times not to put her fingers down there," Mike said. She stuck her hand in the machine, cried out, and pulled back a bloody mess. Blood was running all over her, and the bones were sticking out. "I almost died just looking at it. How anybody could say that I cut up my wife after that. . . ."

Woody helped Mike get Pat to the nearest hospital, nineteen miles from the campground in Mendota, Illinois. Michael thought Mendota had the best hospital he had ever seen. The doctor there put about 300 stitches in Pat's hand, and two of her fingers had to be grafted back on. The Giangrandes made three or four trips to Mendota within the next couple of weeks. The Mendota doctor wrote three or four pages of instructions for Pat's doctor in Chicago on how to take the stitches out. That was a very delicate operation. Still, one of the fingers didn't grow back properly and had to be rebroken. There was nothing either doctor could do. "That depressed her a lot," Michael said. "After a certain time she knew that she would go for the rest of her life with her hand deformed." For months afterward, Pat wore a large bandage and sometimes a rubber glove. Long after her hand was healed she used it to elicit sympathy.

Ed Norris said that during the last couple of years of her life he never saw her hand. Pat's arm was usually bandaged from her fingertips to her shoulder. Sometimes, he said, she wore a sling.

In 1979, Michael and Pat Giangrande were remarried in a religious ceremony at St. Symphorosa's, where the kids went to school. Pat had obtained an official annulment of her marriage to Ed Norris from the Archdiocese of Chicago. Some months earlier, Pat went to court and had the children's names legally changed from Norris to Giangrande, though there was no adoption proceeding. Woody became Michael Giangrande, Jr. (Ed did not know about this, he said, until after Pat's death.) Michael thought perhaps these things would make his wife feel more secure. But she seemed just as nervous and crazy as ever.

● ● ●

Patricia Giangrande was loved in spite of herself. People who knew her before her death have very little to say about her that's truly awful. Michael kept his problems with her to himself and never complained to friends or family. Geraldine Giangrande liked Pat and has never uttered a disparaging word. "If she was a bad person, you can't prove it by me," she said. "By me she was always on her best behavior. She liked me too; she told me that I was the only person who never got on her back. I said, 'I'm not going to come into your house and tell you how to run the place. My son is old enough to take care of himself. I have a hard enough time leading my own life.' I don't like to butt my nose into someone else's family."

"It was never the big things that got to my wife; it was the little things," Michael Giangrande said. "She could reason with the big things. The kids loved her and hated her, the same way it was in her family. Not that they are happy to see her gone. My wife wanted the best for the kids, though she definitely would have been better off without kids. She would call them 'stupid, crazy, dummy,' and those words were the nice words. Our Andrea, my youngest, . . . my wife surprised me with her. I thought she thought four kids were enough, but she made sure she'd get pregnant. She was afraid if she didn't have one of my own kids I might have left her.

"But I would never have left her anyway. . . . I was madly in love with my wife. I put up with her for eight years. Sometimes I lie in bed up in that cell and I feel hate . . . not for what she did to me . . . but for what she did to herself. . . ." Michael had to stop talking because he was crying.

● ● ●

On Tuesday, September 4, 1979—the day after Labor Day—a Mr. Orley Hutchinson called police and said that the day before, near the Venture store in Matteson, he had found a K-Mart check-cashing card issued to Patricia Giangrande. Police asked the management of the Venture store for a list of employees, requesting also that the files be checked to see if anyone had attempted to use the card with Patricia Giangrande's name on it. They also asked for an employee list at the clothing store next door to the Venture. No criminal records came to light. A state police trooper reported that a bag of clothing had been found near the soybean field where the body had been discovered. He thought it might be connected, but it wasn't.

Kankakee County sheriff's policemen Bill Marks and Ed Jackson visited Michael Giangrande at his home on Parkside. Mike had taken a two-week leave of absence from Griffith to straighten out his affairs since the death of his wife. He gave the police Pat's charge account numbers and her checking account number. He reiterated that she left with the two boxes and a makeup bag, with her dentures in place. The police repeated the story Laura Diane had told them about Pat's girlfriend and the girlfriend's boyfriend and the sexual blackmail. "Mr. Giangrande seemed to be quite nervous about this information and said that his daughter must have misunderstood what he was talking about and dismissed the matter with no further conversation," they reported. Michael repeated that he left the house for three hours on the Saturday before the body was found, and he told the policemen where he went. He told them Pat had been a cocktail waitress, she had injured her hand in Woodhaven, and she sometimes wore a rubber glove to protect the bandage. The police asked him if he had the rubber glove, and he went to the basement and brought back a turquoise glove that looked as though it had never been used. Mike said that Pat had been wearing a purple blouse and beige slacks when she left the house that night. He didn't know about her shoes. He repeated the story of the aggravated battery incident at the single parents' picnic in Schiller Park.

The police asked Michael Giangrande if he would like to take a lie detector test, and Michael said he would like to call his attorney first. Michael had retained Paul Bradley the week before because his brother Mark, a student at Kent College of Law, had advised him to get a lawyer when he heard that the house had been searched without Michael's being there. "My advice to him was to cooperate with the investigation in terms of things like what she was wearing, but if they started to interrogate in an accusatorial manner, he should call," Bradley explained. "So in September Jackson and Marks find a box of old clothes in the general area where the body was recovered; they ask Mike if they were hers. Mike says they're not hers, and then they say, 'Oh, by the way, Mike, would you submit to a lie detector test?' "

Bradley talked to the police on the phone and asked them if there was any particular reason why they wanted Michael to take a lie detector test. The police, according to Bradley, acted like it was routine, something Michael should do just to "clear himself." Bradley told them he didn't see why Mike should have to "clear himself" if he was not a suspect. Bradley asked that the next time the police wanted to interrogate his client they notify him so he could be present during the questioning.

The police went to Ed Norris's house after they talked to Michael, but Norris wasn't home. While they were driving back to Kankakee, Jackson and Marks got word that Patricia Giangrande's credit cards had been recovered by a garbageman in an alley near the Giangrande home. The next day the two policemen returned to Chicago, picked up photocopies of the credit cards from the local authorities, and investigated some phone numbers of insurance companies they found in Mrs. Giangrande's telephone book. Jackson talked to a secretary at the State Farm Insurance office who said that the Giangrandes had had an insurance policy for their cars with State Farm. Since 1977 there had been nine claims, most of them for automobile accidents in which Patricia Giangrande was at fault. The policy had been canceled early in 1979.

Ed Norris was home that afternoon. He said that on the night of Saturday, August 25, he had been drinking and watching television at a bar near his house from about 5:30 until about 10:00 P.M. He said that he had called the Giangrande house that night at nine o'clock and that Laura Diane had told him her father was at the racetrack. He told police that Pat worked in bars when they were married and that her first child had been taken away from her. He said that he had been informed by a friend that the insurance policies for Pat

Giangrande had her Aunt Jean named as beneficiary. Norris told the police that Michael Giangrande had been employed as a meat cutter at A&P and had been laid off when the plant closed down. He told a story about Michael losing his temper and getting into a fight at the plant, saying that was the reason he was not hired back when the warehouse reopened. Authorities at A&P later denied this. Jackson and Marks asked Norris if he would take a lie detector test, and he said he would be happy to do so.

Jackson called Bradley back and asked him why he was not allowing his client to take a lie detector test. Bradley told him he didn't see any reason why Michael should have to. "He's the husband of the deceased." Jackson made the statistical point that husbands kill their wives more frequently than anybody else. Bradley countered that other people kill people's wives too and added that he didn't trust polygraph examinations anyway. Jackson said that Bradley could have Michael tested by the Chicago police or by a private firm, if that would be more convenient. Bradley refused.

Bradley says there were other reasons he did not want the test, reasons that he didn't mention to the police. First and foremost, he thinks lie detector tests are a sloppy excuse for real police work. "Why bother having an investigation at all if polygraphs are so great?" he said—"Just give everybody a test." Polygraphs are, in Bradley's opinion, highly unreliable. A guilty man can pass with flying colors, and an innocent person can flunk. "Mike was still in pretty bad shape at the time, taking tranquilizers and so forth. If he got an inconclusive or failed, it would have been very hard on him psychologically. Of course at the time I refused the test, I thought the murder was still being investigated. It wasn't until later that I found out that as soon as the cops found out that Michael had been a meat cutter the investigation stopped."

The investigation didn't really stop at that point, but not much else turned up after Ed Norris told the police where Michael Giangrande used to work. After Jackson and Marks talked to Bradley the second time, they visited Pat's girlfriend. She seemed to know very little about her "best friend." She said they had gone to grammar school together, but she knew nothing about Pat's having boyfriends or taking drugs.

Jackson and Marks interviewed the sanitation worker who said he found the credit cards in a can; it was the Tuesday after Labor Day, he said, and the cards were shoved about a third of the way down.

The can was in the 5600 block of West 64th Street—near the Giangrandes' home but closer to Ed Norris's house. The police visited Marge Russell, now seventy-five years old, who told them Pat abused her first child, but everybody got along fine. She got along with Pat. Michael got along with Pat. Next they visited Joe and Adeline Lakomiak. They learned nothing new from the Lakomiaks.

At 11:00 the next morning, a Thursday, Marks and Jackson visited the neighbor who supposedly had threatened to kill the entire Giangrande family. He denied it. Then they visited the A&P warehouse on Kildare and spoke to the plant manager. He said he recalled that Michael Giangrande had been an employee there at the time they were still cutting meat at the plant. He probably would not have had access to any knives or handsaws while he was working at the plant, the manager said, but it was possible. He said any other inquiries would have to be directed to the personnel office in Des Plaines. Jackson called the office, and a secretary there told him it was difficult to get information dating back three or four years. The following Monday, Jackson called A&P again and urged them to keep looking. Then he talked to the Chicago police about scheduling a lie detector test for Ed Norris. He called Norris at work and at home and got no answer. He was unable to reach Norris all afternoon, so he canceled the appointment for the test. He called a Blake-Lamb undertaker, who told him that Michael seemed to be under the influence of heavy medication during the funeral and had asked while the arrangements were being made if the police had found Pat's hands.

The next morning Jackson received a call from the Chicago Police Department. They said that Ed Norris had made an appointment with them to take a lie detector test.

At 1:30 that afternoon, Jackson and Marks went to Michael Giangrande's home.

"Mr. Giangrande was informed of his Miranda rights by Sergeant Marks verbally," the police report says. "Mr. Giangrande stated that he knew his rights. Sergeant Marks then explained to Mr. Giangrande that much time and effort had been put into the investigation of the homicide of his wife and that the information would be released to the news media with regard to the fact that he had refused to take a polygraph examination and that it had been discovered that he worked as a meat cutter for the A&P Company for many years. It was also explained to Mr. Giangrande that this information was being given to him so that he might consider it in his decision not to take a polygraph examination. While at Mr. Giangrande's residence, he stated that on the previous night someone had attempted to break into the back door and someone had dented the front door of his residence. Mr. Giangrande stated that he had reported this to the Chicago Police. . . . Mr. Giangrande stated that he would contact his attorney and would discuss the matter of the polygraph with him again and would call investigating officers if he had a change of mind. When Reporting Detectives stated that they knew that Mr. Giangrande had been a meat cutter, Mr. Giangrande stated that he wasn't a meat cutter, but had been a 'boner.' "

Michael reported the conversation to Bradley.

"What gets to me," said Bradley, "is the cops kept going out and spreading rumors instead of investigating. Jackson and Marks told Michael that they would tell the newspapers if he refused to take a lie detector test. So I called the police and said, 'Did you contact my client directly and did you tell him that you'd tell the newspapers if he refused to take a lie detector test?' and the cops said they had. I asked them if they didn't think they were opening themselves up for some potential legal problem. The next thing I know, the *Southtown Economist* prints this story with a headline on it something like 'Husband of Murder Victim Refuses Lie Detector Test.' If you read the article, it sounded like this guy killed his wife and why aren't the police charging him with murder?"

After the police talked to Michael Giangrande again, they were notified that Norris had canceled his polygraph test on the advice of his attorney. The next morning, the police received a call from the corporate offices of A&P; a company official said that they found records confirming that Michael Giangrande had worked there from June 17, 1957, until January of 1973 and that he had been a meat cutter.

The investigation of Pat Giangrande's murder was dropped until September 26, when Jackson and Marks called on Geraldine Giangrande. She told them she couldn't understand why Michael had refused a lie detector test and that Pat and Mike seemed to have a good relationship. They spoke to Ed Norris in the afternoon and asked him again to take a lie detector test. He said he would talk to his lawyer about it.

"They kept calling me and harassing me," Norris said. "I finally decided there was no point in me not taking the lie detector test if it would help clear the case up. I passed with flying colors.

"I had mentioned to the police more or less in passing that Giangrande had been a meat cutter at A&P. The police didn't react at all. They just continued their line of questioning, taking notes and whatever. Right away, I felt that the way she died and Giangrande's previous occupation were connected. You see, you probably would have had to live with this person for an extended period of time to realize the type of person you were dealing with in the situation. My ex-wife? Myself, I probably would have murdered her if I stayed married to her. She was that kind of person. You could never reason with her. It wasn't any different being married to him or being married to me. She just changed partners. It was the same constant turmoil.

"My oldest daughter will have nothing to do with me because I told the police that he was a meat cutter and because I wouldn't lie to the police about his being out that Saturday night. I have no animosity towards him, but, at the same time, I wasn't going to lie for him."

Bradley said: "Overall, the obvious worst thing about this case was the coincidence of her being cut up and that he was at one time a meat cutter. That was the reason I said to him all along, 'If you did it, please tell me.' With Patricia Giangrande's history, she was the walking definition of provocation. Had he done it, he might have gotten off with probation on a manslaughter charge. But he didn't do it, and he wouldn't lie and say that he had."

• • •

A coroner's inquest into the death of Patricia Giangrande was convened at 3:30 on the afternoon of November 27. Very little new or different turned up at the inquest. Jackson explained why the autopsy report indicated that the boxes had not been in the field for too long a time before being found—because no dew had collected on the boxes. Dr. Shalgos said that the cuts were clean and were all made at the joints, but he did not feel that they were made by a person with surgical expertise. At the inquest, the year 1975—the date Michael Giangrande said he stopped working for A&P—was given as the correct date, rather than 1973, which showed up in the police report.

It was noted that there was an injury on the right side of Pat Giangrande's face near her eye and that the cause of death was unknown.

A grand jury was convened on Monday, January 14. Charles Hartman, an assistant state's attorney, told the jury that he was seeking a true bill against Michael Giangrande, a murder indictment, and that he was also investigating the possibility of an accomplice. He gave his reasons: The medical examiner, Dr. Shalgos, said that the body was cut up very neatly. It was not hacked up, but cut through the flesh with some sharp instrument, a knife, and sawed through the bone—a very neat job. The victim's husband was a meat cutter, Hartman continued. One of the boxes came out of the house in which Patricia lived with her husband. Hartman cited the bloody rubber bags, the gloves, and traces of hair that were found with the body; the hair was "morphologically similar" to Michael Giangrande's hair.

Kankakee County police officers Tim Nugent, Ed Jackson, and Bill Marks; two Chicago homicide detectives; a canine unit; and the media, including a reporter from Channel 2 with a camera crew, converged on the Giangrande residence on Parkside on Saturday morning, January 19. They had a search warrant. Michael Giangrande and his children were escorted from the house and the police went inside. They secured nineteen items of evidence, including a spot of blood on the bed frame and a piece of stained carpet from the bedroom. Quite likely, the blood belonged to Patricia Giangrande. The stained carpet was found to contain oil of paprika. Most of the items were insignificant. For instance, the police took some plastic bags with tape on the edges; Michael said he had used them for painting. The tape had a rust-colored stain on it. The stain was not tested.

Michael was taken into custody, and the kids were temporarily turned over to the Department of Children and Family Services. The grand jury returned the murder indictment the following Monday, January 21. Bond was set at $100,000, so $10,000 would get Michael released from jail pending trial. He went home to 6040 Parkside Avenue on Thursday, the 24th.

●   ●   ●

The halls of justice, as they stand at 26th and California, are dingy and spacious and vaguely depressing. The ceilings are so high and the corridors so wide that any attempts at uniform heating, cooling, or illumination are bound to be in vain. But, despite its drawbacks, the physical presence of the place commands a measure of respect, the kind of respect accorded many old government buildings, libraries, monuments, and theaters. These are places where lives are altered, decisions are made, and a society's culture is reflected. The courthouse does not cater to the middle class the way an institution like traffic court does. Few middle-class people see the inside of the Criminal Courts Building. The crowd here is a curious mix of classes: poor, lower-class folk who have been accused of a crime in this county; have been victimized by one, or whose friends or relatives have been accused or victimized; and, on the other side, the lawyers and judges, upper-middle-class people striving to be high class, dressed for court, looking prosperous—it doesn't matter whether they represent the state or the defense; they are members of the same club.

Michael Giangrande and his parents and friends seem out of place here. (The first day of the trial, Mrs. Giangrande's wallet was taken from her purse while she sat in the courtroom.) It is the court of Judge Thomas Maloney, on the sixth floor of the building. The high-ceilinged corridor seems strangely quiet. A couple of months earlier, John Gacy was tried across the hall from Maloney's court, and the place was teeming with reporters all the time. Now there is nobody around, especially in the afternoon, after the continuances have been granted and sentences handed down.

The 22nd of April, a Tuesday, is freakishly warm. The potential jurors sit, their badges pasted to their breast pockets, on the right side of the room, with a foot or two left between them, waiting to be called to the jury box. Judge Maloney sits in front of the room. His hand supports his forehead, giving generous display to a shock of curly, silver hair. He has a wide, round face and wears dark-rimmed glasses that give him the appearance of an owl. Maloney studies sheets passed to him by the bailiff as the bailiff calls names. The judge asks the jurors about their line of work, their family's occupations, why they may or may not sit on this jury that will try a man for a gruesome homicide. The attorneys, two male and female pairs, sit at two tables set in an *L* shape. The prosecutors from Bernard Carey's office, Lorna Propes and Charles Hartman, face Judge Maloney on the bench. The prosecution is physically closer to the jury, but the defense team, Cornelia Tuite and Paul Bradley, face the jurors directly. Michael Giangrande, a wiry man dressed in a green suit, white shirt, and thin tie, with wire-rimmed glasses and dark hair that is starting to thin on top, leans back in the leather chair and holds his hand with fingers across his mouth. He sits next to Cornelia and occasionally whispers to her. Psychologically, Bradley says, it is good for the jury to see a woman about the same age as the victim talking to and vaguely touching the defendant.

The lawyers make notes and confer quietly as each juror tells his story. Finally, there are twelve people sitting in the box who are qualified as far as Judge Maloney is concerned. Now the lawyers start weeding them out. One has too many friends and relatives who are police officers; one seems too petty, another too anxious, another too angry that he has never been chosen to sit on a jury before. Finally the lawyers settle on four women and eight men: a single north-suburban man in his forties who wears a beard and jogs; a beautiful, near-north-side Carly Simon lookalike; a steel worker who has been laid off. Lorna Propes will comment later that Michael Giangrande was tried by his peers, *really* tried by his peers. In age they were his peers, and the majority of them were men. They were, she will say, "a jury pretty much like him that could relate to his situation."

Two female alternates are selected, and the court is satisfied. The judge adjourns, saying the opening statements will be heard the next day. Walking from the courtroom with his parents, on the first leg of the journey back to his empty house on Parkside Avenue, Michael Giangrande says that it's the first day in nine months that he's been calm. At 5:00 P.M., the temperature is eighty-eight degrees.

The next day is sunny, but the temperature has dropped thirty degrees. The prosecutors wheel in their evidence on gray metal carts; one of the carts has an old sticker on the side that clearly says "Gacy." The carts have trays on top that contain files, little boxes, a portfolio of color pictures, capsules with laboratory specimens. The prosecutors carry in two easels that stand about six feet high and a couple of cardboard charts measuring roughly four by five. One is a map showing the Giangrande house and the spot where the boxes were found; another is a floor plan of the house. The prosecutors also haul in a blank pad of drawing paper and the boxes; the toilet paper box that they will refer to as the "torso" box and the smaller potato chip box that contained the head and limbs. They have a Colony Foods bag, an economy-sized box that once was full of laundry detergent, and a large, industrial-sized clear plastic bag filled with other crumpled-up plastic bags with tape on the edges. On one section of this tape there is a reddish substance. Michael Giangrande says it's paint; the police will later testify that the stain has not been tested. But the stain looks like blood—and it will lie conspicuously on the floor in the middle of the courtroom throughout the trial, even though it is irrelevant to the trial.

Hartman, dressed in a dark, pinstriped, three-piece suit, and Propes, immaculate in a pastel coat and skirt and coordinated blouse, are messing around with the dilapidated boxes and the trash from the Giangrandes' garage and basement. It is an odd contrast.

The defense has no such paraphernalia, but the defense theoretically does not have to prove anything. The prosecution has to prove that Michael Giangrande killed his wife—though they don't know the cause of her death, or where it took place—beyond a reasonable doubt.

Both opening statements are low-key and to the point. Bradley asks the jury to avoid compounding the tragedy of Patricia Giangrande's death by adding to it the tragedy of convicting an innocent man of murder. The other side insists that the weight of the evidence will show that Michael Giangrande is not a victim but a perpetrator. The state begins by setting up a map showing the relationship between the Giangrande house and the bean field in Kankakee County. The state implies that, if you live in Michael Giangrande's neighborhood near Midway Airport, the bean field is a logical place to go if you want to dump a body. You would, the prosecution thinks, drive straight down Cicero Avenue until you got to a rural area where you might think no one would find the body for months. Had you been Michael Giangrande, the prosecutors suppose, this bean field just outside the city would appear remote. The defense counters by superimposing a sheet of acetate over the state's map to show that there are half a dozen routes to the bean field from the south side of the city, that the field is not far from Interstate 57, the main north-south artery that cuts through Illinois. The place is accessible and may or may not appear remote to any number of people, Bradley implies.

On Thursday the 24th, exactly eight months since Pat Giangrande's disappearance, the state calls the head cashier from the Colony Foods store on West 63rd Street. The cashier identifies Patricia Giangrande's check-cashing card and says that a check was cashed—the card was used—on the day before she disappeared, August 23.

The weather outside has turned bleak. The temperature is in the

Kathy Lee Lynn testifies about the refrigerator. Michael's mother tells what she knows. Laura Diane is called. She gives her version of what happened in the hours before her mother left. She says that her stepfather was home all weekend except for a few hours on Saturday night. Lorna Propes questions Laura Diane about the boxes. Laura Diane, a slight, blond teenager, now pauses after some of the questions, as though considering them anew. She says she doesn't remember if she took toilet paper out of the box before she brought it upstairs. Lorna Propes asks her about the rubber gloves. The prosecution wants to know where her mother kept them and why she couldn't produce them right away. There are a lot of things Laura Diane doesn't remember. Propes asks her about physical fights she may have had with her mother. Bradley objects, saying that she is confusing the witness. Laura Diane looks around, as though she's bewildered. Propes asks Laura Diane about her father's story that her mother had been drugged and forced to perform sex acts with her girlfriend's boyfriend. Bradley objects on the grounds that it's hearsay. The matter goes no further. Laura Diane has not been a good witness. It seems, for one reason or another, as though she isn't telling the truth.

Woody, also known as Michael Antonio Giangrande, Jr., turns out to be a star witness. He also tells the story of what happened that night and in the days following. A small fourteen-year-old with a pixie face, he is very sure of himself. He gives the exact time of the rinse cycle on the dishwasher. Lorna Propes cross-examines, dwelling on what Woody heard while he was in bed, while his mother was yelling. She tries to get him to say that he heard the door slam twice, implying that his mother left and came back. Woody stands his ground. He insists he heard the door close and the car drive away and that's all. Woody compensates for Laura Diane.

Michael Giangrande takes the stand in his own behalf. He shows very little emotion as he answers Bradley's questions about the time he spent in cosmetology school, his jobs at A&P, his marriage. He details briefly what happened before Pat left the house and what he did over the weekend subsequent to her departure. He explains where the meat hooks and the knives that were found in his house came from originally. He says that the suitcases Marks saw in the basement were full of junk. In the cross, Propes asks him about the credit cards. Michael Giangrande doesn't know how the credit cards got in the garbage can a few blocks from his house. He says he didn't kill his wife. Michael Giangrande is the last witness for the defense.

The rebuttals are heard on Wednesday afternoon. The state puts some of the police officials back on the stand to clarify what the Giangrandes told them originally and to compare those stories with what has been said on the stand. Tim Nugent tells the court that Laura Diane never mentioned anything about oil of paprika when she was originally questioned about the argument her parents had. Bradley manages to cast some doubt on the facts in the original police report, comparing the testimony of the police officers to what was actually written in their report. Lorna Propes calls an official from WMAQ who testifies that "Saturday Night Live" aired at 11:39 P.M. on Saturday, August 25, instead of the customary 10:30 slot, implying that Michael had lied originally about what time he returned home that night.

Chuck Hartman gives the state's first closing arguments, recounting the testimony about the physical evidence. After that, both Paul Bradley and Lorna Propes argue their positions persuasively. Bradley hesitates to overstate his case. He emphasizes that all the evidence is circumstantial and says that, in order to believe that Michael Giangrande killed his wife, you must believe that the children were in on it. You have to believe that Michael Giangrande is some kind of Houdini, in fact, who managed to put his wife's car in a parking lot at a Venture store without being detected and dispose of an awful, bloody mess without ever leaving a trace. Michael Giangrande would have had to cut his wife apart with a power saw without attracting the attention of any of his neighbors and then dispose of the saw. Bradley pleads with the jury not to take the matter any further, to let Michael Giangrande go home, to give him his children back so they can build a new life.

Lorna Propes is also compelling. She wants to know who but Michael Giangrande might have done it. There is no other evidence to implicate anyone else to the slightest extent. (The other "torso murders" did not come to light in the trial.) She emphasizes that Michael was a meat cutter. She implies that Laura Diane is not trustworthy, that Laura Diane is lying. She points out that Woody is currently living with Michael Giangrande's parents, that he may not be lying but may be confused.

By 6:30 P.M. it is all over and the jury is sent out. Cornelia Tuite, Paul Bradley, Michael Giangrande, the prosecutors, reporters, and attorneys who have stopped in to watch the closing arguments move in clusters out of the courtroom and down the street to Jean's Restaurant, where they wait for the jury to come back with a verdict or for 9:30 P.M., when the jury will quit deliberating for the night.

Coincidentally, Wednesday, April 30, is Lorna Propes's last day in the state's attorney's office, so there is a kind of celebration going on at the bar section of Jean's, where Lorna and her prosecutor colleagues are sitting and standing. The bar section is separated from the restaurant by a tightly woven screen. At a table, Michael, Cornelia, and Paul are having a beer. Michael is smoking and biting his fingernails. Paul has a cigar. Cornelia orders something to eat. Paul thinks that the shorter the time the jury is out, the better chance that the verdict has gone in the defense's favor. He points out that the jury is going to have dinner, then they have to elect a foreman, so it will be a little while, at least. Michael says that his friends and family are planning a party for him at a bowling alley in his neighborhood. He wonders why everyone else is so nervous. "I'm the one that might not be going home tonight," he says. Paul says that he doesn't want to talk about that possibility. Michael says that Paul's closing argument was excellent. He reiterates his faith in Bradley's skill as a lawyer. Lorna Propes gets half a dozen phone calls during the next hour and a half. None of them are from Judge Maloney's court.

Prosecutor Chuck Hartman walks by the table where Cornelia and Paul are sitting with Michael. Paul introduces Michael to Hartman, and they shake hands cordially. Hartman says, "I don't know whether you killed your wife or not, but I believe that there is a God." Michael agrees that he too believes in God and hopes that the truth will out. Chuck wishes him luck. Michael says: "I understand that you are only doing your job." Jean's Restaurant is filling with lawyers who are drinking and growing more boisterous. At about 8:30, Lorna Propes tells Paul Bradley that she and some friends of hers are going to another restaurant; she makes arrangements to call him as soon as she hears anything. At 9:00 P.M., Bradley, Tuite, and Giangrande prepare to go back to the courtroom, expecting to be told that the jury is going to retire for the night.

While the clusters of lawyers move back to the courtroom, several phone calls go out from Maloney's court.

The jury has arrived at a verdict. Paul and Cornelia hear the news from the bailiff when they get back to the sixth floor at about 9:15. One of the bailiffs shakes his head, no, at Cornelia. The judge takes his seat on the bench. The jury files into the jury box. They will not look at the defense table. A crowd of prosecutors—late of the celebration for Lorna Propes—enters the courtroom. Though they've been called away from dinner, they are smiling, laughing, and talking loudly. Michael Giangrande's parents are sitting in the room, holding hands. Some of the Giangrande nieces and nephews and Michael's sister Marge are there as well. The judge asks the foreman of the jury, the Carly Simon lookalike, to hand the verdict over to the bailiff. "Guilty as charged," the bailiff says flatly.

There is an audible sigh in the room. Two guards move toward Michael, who's sitting with Bradley and Cornelia Tuite at the defense table. Michael stands up, takes his keys and his wallet from his pockets, and hands them to Bradley. He approaches the bench with his lawyers; the prosecutors approach the bench. Judge Maloney sets sentencing for May 29. He denies bail and orders that Michael Giangrande be held in Cook County Jail prior to sentencing. Geraldine Giangrande stands up and watches him go. She is crying, as are one of Michael's nephews and some of the female friends of the family.

On the way out, Michael asks Cornelia to look after his mother. Cornelia tells Mike that his mother is a strong person and she will be all right. The Giangrandes leave the courtroom and head for the parking lot across the street. Paul Bradley tells Michael's parents that he thinks there's a very good case for appeal. The prosecutors are still in the courtroom laughing loudly. Geraldine Giangrande is leaning on a cane, standing in front of the Criminal Courts Building, as the jurors file quietly out of the building and walk toward their cars on the other side of California.

When Paul Bradley got drunk a couple hours later, he broke down and sobbed.

● ● ●

All the physical evidence in the case against Michael Giangrande, all the physical evidence connected to the dead, bloodless, dismembered body of Patricia Giangrande, apparently originated at the Giangrande home. The plastic bags containing the body pieces were the same as the plastic bags found in the basement. The tape matched. The boxes—one of them just the right size to hold a torso—had come from the basement. The baby's T-shirt found near the body was similar to babies' T-shirts found in the Giangrande basement in the January search. Two bloody rubber gloves found at the bean field—one more worn than the other—were similar to a single glove that Michael turned over to the police the week after the funeral. The difference was that the glove the defendant turned over to the police had never been used, and previously Laura Diane had been unable to produce any gloves at all. This suggested that perhaps a new pair of gloves had been purchased when the Giangrandes discovered the police were interested in rubber gloves.

It was also suggested that the drop of blood found on the bed frame had been missed in a cleanup operation, that the missing piece of carpet may or may not have contained oil of paprika, that there were so many clothes remaining in the bedroom that Patricia Giangrande could not possibly have taken two boxes of clothes with her when she left. By using the map, the prosecutors proposed that, when Michael Giangrande went out on Saturday night, he headed straight south and dumped the body in a place he considered a remote area. The state apparently thinks—and the jury apparently agrees—that Michael Giangrande killed his wife sometime Friday (the pathologist's estimated time of death), then cut her up, packed her in boxes, dumped the boxes in the bean field Saturday night, disposed of the tools he used, cleaned up the mess, and parked her car in the Venture store lot sometime between the time of the dismemberment and Monday afternoon. The credit cards he threw in the garbage later.

But no one ever proposed a theory as to *how* Patricia Giangrande was killed and cut into sections, by Michael Giangrande or by anybody else, for that matter. Nor did anyone say *when,* with any sort of clear timetable. Or *where,* with any physical evidence in the house, basement, or garage that Patricia Giangrande had been butchered and packaged in plastic bags and cardboard boxes. The state never presented a plausible explanation for the crime. It disturbed me. It still does.

Lorna Propes, who was and is totally convinced that Michael Giangrande killed his wife and cut her up, said: "The evidence was so strong and pointed at him so directly and so exclusively that I felt it was overwhelming." Lorna Propes also wondered where the viable theory was, but she never felt it incumbent upon her to present it. She thought that Bradley would have presented a viable *alternative* theory if he had been able to. Propes, who is in private practice now, said that each bit of evidence could be explained away—like the fact that Pat Giangrande packed her clothes in two boxes, one of them just about the right size for a torso—but that the cumulative effect was just too much. She cited the hair analysis, the credit cards in the trash a few blocks away, the absence of sexual assault. "It can't all be explained," she said. "It's just too coincidental to say that all of this could have happened to poor Michael Giangrande."

Lorna Propes made little of the evidence that Giangrande used to be a meat cutter, though Bradley thought that fact had more to do with the conviction of Michael Giangrande than anything else. Bradley thought that Michael Giangrande did not receive a fair trial and that there was insufficient evidence in the first place. "The state never proved that a murder was committed," he said. "My interpretation of the evidence is the state said he killed her in a single-family home with five children present and cut her up with a saw between 6:30 and 9:00 P.M. that Friday night. They never proved how he did it. There was no evidence how he did it. There was never any proof of venue. [The crime—whatever crime was committed—may not have been committed in Chicago.] The jury was asked to speculate.

"Society doesn't like to admit that there are crimes which can't be solved. There are crimes that are virtually unsolvable. If I got on an elevator in this building between five and six o'clock and stabbed someone and came back to my office, no one would ever be able to solve that crime. They couldn't charge me simply because I was here and I was strong enough to do it. Ninety percent of burglaries in the city are never solved. Murder is obviously more urgent. The police want to make an arrest, and the police are more likely, in that case, to make a mistake." Bradley was appealing the conviction.

●   ●   ●

On Thursday morning, May 29, Michael Giangrande was sentenced to sixty years in jail, a heavy sentence that Judge Maloney justified by citing the brutality and heinousness of the crime. At the time of sentencing, Michael didn't know where any of the children were. The three youngest girls were in a foster home somewhere. He had no idea about Laura Diane, and he suspected Woody was with Ed Norris. The appeal would take at least nine months. In the meantime, Michael Giangrande had lost his house, his car, his job, and his kids. He sat in a maximum security cell in Menard Correctional Facility twenty-three hours a day.

At least one Saturday a month, Vito and Geraldine Giangrande took a special commercial bus from the south side of Chicago to the downstate prison about seven hours away. Geraldine would prepare a bag lunch, and they would spend a few hours in the afternoon visiting together.

●   ●   ●

For some months after Michael Giangrande left for Menard, I was haunted by something he had said to me one afternoon while he was in Cook County Jail awaiting sentencing. I had asked him if he had any idea who killed his wife. He said he did have an idea, but he did not want to mention a name because "I don't want anybody to have to go through what I've been through." The absence of anger in the face of injustice and the lack of desire to see the "real" murderer captured struck me as odd. (The only explanation I could come up with was that Michael was planning some secret revenge he did not want to tell me about.) What made his answer sound even weirder to me, however, was that I knew I had heard that answer before, in another context.

Searching through newspaper clippings some time later, I ran across some material about Patty Columbo. A number of years before Patricia Giangrande's murder, Patty Columbo and her boyfriend had killed Patty's parents and teenage brother. At the time of her trial, Patty was a sexy, blonde, twenty-one-year-old, and some lurid evidence was presented that showed Patty would have done just about anything to get somebody to kill her family. In addition to her sexual exploits, Patty made maps of the family home for would-be assassins and promised money from her inheritance. She also procured weapons. But nothing quite worked out. Finally, she and her boyfriend had to commit the murders themselves. The killings were brutal and bloody. One of the police officials came away from the scene of the crime, the family home, saying he had never seen anything like it. It was established that Patty had stabbed her brother repeatedly, almost beyond recognition. Through the entire investigation and trial, Patty Columbo maintained her innocence. Even in newspaper interviews with her after the conviction, she insisted that she was very close to her family and would never have done such a thing. When a reporter asked her who she thought might have murdered her family, she declined to answer. She said she would not want another person who might be innocent to have to go through the hell she had been through. Instead, her anger, like Mike Giangrande's anger, was directed at the state lawyers who had railroaded her into prison, rather than at the "real killer" who had gone free.

●   ●   ●

On September 9, 1981, a three-judge panel—William S. White, Dom J. Rizzi, and Daniel J. McNamara—in the Illinois First District Appellate Court reversed the verdict in the Giangrande case and remanded the matter for a new trial. The judges said that there was enough circumstantial evidence to warrant a conviction, but because of some misstatements by the prosecution and other mistakes, Michael had not received a fair trial. On November 30, the state's petition for a rehearing of the appeal was denied, and the case was thrown back into Judge Maloney's hands. Technically, Michael was now eligible for release on bail, but, in actuality, this would take some time. Michael got out of prison at the end of May 1982, and he moved in with his parents in Evergreen Park. Laura Diane was still in a foster home, but Woody, Adrian, and Lisa were living with their father in the duplex on Long. Ed Norris was unemployed. He and Woody, who had changed his name back to Ed Norris, Jr., and the girls were living on Social Security payments the kids received because their mother was dead. Michael got temporary custody of his daughter, Andrea.

Michael managed to support himself and stay out of trouble until the following December, when he tried to pick up a woman near the Rush Street area. Thinking she was a prostitute, Mike offered her $20 to allow him to perform a sex act on her. The woman was an undercover cop who identified herself and arrested him. Michael was fined $50 and ordered to pay $30 in court costs.

●   ●   ●

Geraldine Giangrande died on June 24, 1983. Michael wrote me a letter: "No one knows better than I what a great loss my mother is to me. I miss her terribly. I thank God that I had a year to spend with her before she died. At times I believe that it was God's will that I received my first reversal so that I could be with her for that year. At least that is what I like to believe. As far as the rest of my family goes, when my mother died, they died with her. I can only surmise that they want to have nothing to do with me." Soon afterward, Mike met a south suburban woman and fell in love. His fiancée believed in him as unstintingly as his mother had.

Also during that summer, Michael heard from Woody, who wondered if there had been an insurance policy on his mother, money that he and the other children would inherit if Mike was convicted again. In fact, Pat Giangrande had been insured for about $15,000, but the claim was being held up until Michael's appeals were exhausted.

● ● ●

Michael and Paul Bradley returned to Judge Maloney's courtroom to begin selecting a jury for the new trial on December 7, 1983. The prosecuting team was Michael Angorola and Timothy Quinn, who, coincidentally, had been involved in the Patty Columbo case. The Quinn-Angorola prosecution shifted some of the emphasis that Propes and Hartman had placed on certain small facts to other small facts. For instance, Timothy Quinn made mention that "after Patricia was cut up as she was, she was packaged like meat in plastic bags." But the key to the state's case, and the only real difference at the second trial, was Woody's appearance for the state. Ed Norris, Jr., retold the story of the evening with the Lakomiaks. He said that when he went to bed at 11:00 P.M. on that Thursday night, his three younger sisters were asleep in another room. He did not know where his older sister, who shared a bedroom with him, was at the time. His parents, he said, were still out.

He was awakened some time later by voices: Mike, Laura Diane, and his mother were having some kind of an argument. "I could hear them but I couldn't make out what they were saying," Woody testified. "My bedroom door was open, and everything got quiet all of a sudden, and I see my stepfather Mike carrying my ma over his shoulder toward the back of the house. . . . She was wearing a nightgown. . . . They came out of the master bedroom and proceeded toward the back of the house. . . . A few seconds later my sister, Laura, walked toward the back of the house too. . . .

"My mother was kind of like groaning a little. I got out of my bed, and I looked in my parent's bedroom, and I saw a wrench laying on the bed, and I saw a puddle of blood on the bed. . . .

"I went back in my bedroom and got in my bed. I heard my stepfather tell my sister to 'go upstairs and close your bedroom door.'

She did. I laid there for a while and fell back asleep." When Woody woke up the next morning, at about 10:00 A.M., he said, there was no one there but his four sisters.

The prosecutor asked Woody what his feelings toward his mother were when she died. He said, "I didn't love her. I didn't hate her." Despite Paul Bradley's efforts to discredit Woody and imply that he was under pressure from Ed Norris or someone else to lie to the court, Michael was again convicted of murder and taken back to Cook County Jail.

Paul Bradley begged Judge Maloney for leniency when Mike went for sentencing on January 6, 1984. The Judge reduced Michael Giangrande's term from sixty to forty years. Michael, forty-four years old, could possibly have a few healthy years left after he served his term. The conviction, Bradley said, would be appealed.

Like many an intelligent convict, Mike Giangrande has learned quite a lot about the law. He says that he is not sure why Woody said what he said in court, but he has some theories about the pressure Woody was under. He did not testify on his own behalf, he says, because of the legal strategy of his defense. He rejects the idea that he could have refuted Woody's story.

Michael Giangrande claims there are new facts, facts that even Paul Bradley did not know about until after his second trial. "I will only say that if any of it would have been brought out at my trial," Michael writes, "the odds are I would not be in prison today."

• • •

So a plethora of missing facts still surround the peculiar fate of Eugenia Patricia Delgado Teeple Russell Lynn Norris Giangrande, whose hands and upper plate have never been found. In lieu of the truth, there are only suspicions. Suspicions about Laura Diane's role in this bizarre domestic arrangement. Suspicions about why the new facts did not come to light sooner. Suspicions about the nature of love, and memory, and changes over time. Suspicions that maybe Lorna Propes was right when she said, "Juries seldom make mistakes."

Not long ago Paul Bradley mentioned to me that Laura Diane is an emancipated minor now, living somewhere on her own. Very soon she will be the same age her mother was when she gave birth to her first child.

2

Hugh Hefner's First Funeral

At the time Bobbie Arnstein, Hugh Hefner's executive secretary, killed herself, Playboy was flourishing. The magazine had grown from a soft-core pornographic periodical into a philosophical treatise espousing a particular way of life; the corporation that emerged from the magazine had, in turn, spawned a subculture. And in Chicago, the home of Playboy Enterprises and Hugh Hefner, that subculture was a hip, wealthy, even highbrow society that revolved around the Playboy mansion on the city's Gold Coast. Playboy was such a powerful force in the arts and entertainment industry that almost every celebrity who came through town seemed to be here on Playboy's tab. (Playboy funded writers like Paul Tyner, who were down on their luck, and entertainers like Lenny Bruce, who resisted convention and worked outside the mainstream.) Hefner had become very political, pumping money into civil rights and first amendment causes, and he hosted benefits at his home as well as in his clubs and restaurants. It was a heady time when everything Playboy touched seemed to turn to gold.

America was about to witness the end of the halcyon days.

By January 15, 1975, we were doing what felt good, eating birth control pills, reveling in loose attachments. We had decided on healthy, acceptable levels of selfishness, the only cure for chronic unhappiness, sworn enemy of the free spirit.

Hugh M. Hefner had pointed the way. A cultural leftist who made a career out of being true to himself, he worked hard to ride the crest of this wave and so became our hero. He was a nobody from nowhere, a prophet of the flaunted convention and finally a millionaire many times over. The story of how he had built his magazine into an enterprise was media folklore. Hefner was a living legend.

Ironically, much of the excitement of the heady two decades of Playboy's success had dissipated, and Hefner, seeking a quick romantic fix, had lately been touting himself as an F. Scott Fitzgerald character. But he seemed to have forgotten the end of the story. Jay Gatsby had never had a day like this one. The Chicago press could see that Hefner was upset; his face was contorted with pain. This Hefner was enough to make any public relations guy cringe. Not to mention the lawyers, who had already been politely told to go to hell. He had a few words to say about Bobbie Arnstein, his employee and friend, found dead a day ago.

74

We had never seen him so distraught. Several years earlier, Hefner had appeared on the "Dick Cavett Show" in a confrontation with Susan Brownmiller and another feminist, and the two women had thrown him off balance. But this was different. He was physically drained and visibly harried, despite the fact that he had not an enemy in the room.

Hefner had always enjoyed an excellent relationship with the press, especially the local celebrity-starved Chicago press. We reporters gladly accepted his party invitations. We liked his hospitality, his cooperation, and the fact that he funded First Amendment causes. So Hefner was a kind of friend to many people here today—the small legion of journalists packed into the auditorium-sized main room at the mansion on North State Parkway. The lords and ladies of gossip in their cashmere coats. The pressed and polished network news reporters. The scruffy kids from the city desk, who knew this press conference could make page one. The special assignment columnists and the "new journalism" feature writers, scribbling notes about Hefner's clothes and Gallo sculptures and the polished wood paneling in the near north side castle.

Hugh Hefner accused the prosecutors at the office of U.S. Attorney James Thompson of murder. Thompson was then positioning himself as a tough law-and-order man, anticipating the next year's gubernatorial contest. Hefner felt that Thompson was leading "a politically inspired witch hunt." He publicly proclaimed that the federal investigators had manufactured a drug charge against one of his people in a calculated effort to hang a criminal charge on him. Here in the palace hall, above the dimly lit swimming pool fashioned into a tropical paradise, next door to a game room with wall-to-wall pinball machines, Hefner screamed that "the motherfuckers" had killed Bobbie Arnstein, whose body had just been found in the Maryland Hotel. A sealed envelope on the bedstand was marked: "This is another one of those boring suicide notes."

We did not want to see this. And there were those of us who winced and turned away. But there were others who sensed that Hefner's brand of slick hedonism had reached its zenith, that perhaps his celebrity was old hat, that Richard Nixon, Phyllis Schlafly, and Jerry Falwell were here to stay for a while. There were reporters who smelled blood, who claimed to have inside information that the U.S. Attorney's office was indeed after Hefner, and what was more, their sources said, that there was evidence against him. The readers went wild over the Bobbie Arnstein business; the audience always loves it when somebody who is rich and famous gets into trouble, it seems.

It was a good story. There were chuckles among the cynics whom Hugh Hefner had been wining and dining for years. That afternoon they were saying that old Bunnyman looked like he was on something himself. That was the cruelest part of this absurd tableau. That was what Bobbie Arnstein was trying to avoid by writing a suicide note which was tantamount to a press release for Playboy Enterprises as her last act on earth. Friends of Bobbie could almost see her pacing around in her little white office after the scene in the main room, shaking her head and asking, "What is all this shit, anyway?"

● ● ●

Bobbie Arnstein did not understand certain kinds of injustice. She was repeatedly impatient with the bureaucracy that inevitably sprang up at Playboy. "What *is* this?" she was quoted as saying when presented with memoranda, little reminders of policy, evidence of growing corporate paranoia. Teeny, tiny Bobbie, with the Jean Shrimpton face and the Bianca Jagger wardrobe, came on with the funny looks every time some middle manager refused to authorize a $10 raise for a mansion hired hand or clerk.

"You're being outrageous, Bobbie," the person who was making twelve times the amount of the valet, or the chauffeur, or the waiter, or the security guard, or the laundress would admonish her. Bobbie Arnstein would not argue over a few lousy dollars. She loathed the mentality of those who would. Small dishonesties bothered her. She was positively stupid, some say, when it came to that silly pinball machine. The scoreboard had a tendency to roll over too fast when game room sessions stretched to six and eight hours. The machine would heat up, tacking a hundred or a thousand unearned points onto a score already into six figures. Bobbie's fellow players were inclined to let the matter pass, if they noticed it at all. But it was not Bobbie Arnstein's style to collect points that she did not deserve. The amount may have been trivial, but the principle of the matter was not. She could not just let it go by. And neither could her opponents. Because, if they tried, pint-sized Bobbie would stand up there in her platform boots, her leather vest, her feathers and beads and get plain, full-tilt righteous. They would deduct the thousand points from her score, even if she was far and away the front-runner in the game. People who played with Bobbie learned to play fair because that was the way she wanted it. She wanted to get it right. She wanted to be fair, to tell the truth. That's all.

• • •

A group of Playboy executives and hangers-on were eating at an Indian restaurant one night. The waiter, a native Indian recently emigrated to Chicago, could not speak or understand English very well. He was not getting it right and had a difficult time taking food orders from the eight people at the table. He stammered his way around to Bobbie, who stared at him through large tinted lenses. "What would you like, sir?" he asked with some amount of arrogance. Bobbie moved one hand to pull open the left side of her shirt, revealing the fact that she was braless. With the chewed-up edge of her middle finger in the other hand, she forced his attention on some lackluster cleavage. Bobbie Arnstein was thirty-four years old, and she had become accustomed to the hysterical laughter she got following the performance of some social outrage.

Getting a laugh at the expense of a bumbling steward in a restaurant was not really a very nice thing to do. And why would Bobbie Arnstein, then the assistant to the president of Playboy Enterprises, the most important woman at the seventy-four-room mansion, want to pick on some puny waiter? Because he had done the one thing that she could not tolerate. He had not gotten the Anglo-Saxon vocabular distinction between men and women straight. In Bobbie Arnstein's line of work, you were reminded of that distinction often.

Clowning around was a cover for Bobbie. It softened the big dishonesties, the things she rarely talked about, the things that really hurt. When she complained about her salary and title to Hefner, he always laughed, and he thought she was just being funny. She was hilarious when she argued that she was a specialist in his organization, that she understood his moods, his prejudices, his makeup better than anyone else. She wanted to be paid the salary of a specialist, she said. She wanted money to be a signal that she was important to him.

Bobbie Arnstein told her friends that she wanted a title that would define her twenty-four-hour-a-day duties more accurately than the words *executive secretary* did. But after more than ten years of living within breathing space of her boss, she was unable to come right out and tell him what she wanted. It just was not that kind of a relationship. And everybody else she talked to was slowly going deaf on the subject. Hugh Hefner could fix the situation; he could make it right. But the publisher-genius who parlayed $600 into a fortune because he knew what every American male wanted could not see what his handmaiden wanted. She required a monetary pat on the head, a paper reassurance that he really needed her. She was not getting either, and that was one of the reasons she tried to kill herself the first time.

• • •

Bobbie Arnstein used to say that she had not wanted the goddamn job in the first place. Bobbie was a child when she joined the ranks of the Michigan Avenue slaves. She followed a series of low-paying Girl Friday posts at a shoe store, a car dealership, and a radio station, around the north Loop area. An inauspicious career at Lakeview High School on Chicago's north side had not prepared her to tough it out in the secretarial pool. Bobbie was smart and had been railroaded into all the track one classes. Her teachers thought she would make an excellent teacher. By the time her four years were up, Bobbie Arnstein was sick of school. If she ever thought of continuing her education, she kept it a secret.

The market was glutted with sweet young things in the same predicament. But Bobbie Arnstein had a slight edge: she oozed public relations savvy. She had bleached blonde hair, an infectious smile, and brains enough to act sophisticated—all advantages in the customer service racket. A counselor at a local employment agency knew Bobbie was beguiling enough to work at a company with one of the better addresses.

Bobbie Arnstein was first placed at an advertising firm, the most glamorous job open at the moment. She was pretty happy there when the agency called a few weeks later, urging her to look into an offer at Playboy. "This job is *you*, Bobbie," the woman insisted. Bobbie was not so sure. She thought it over and called the woman back. She didn't know if she could measure up physically. There was a mystique about Playboy, and Bobbie thought it might be fun to work there, but she was reluctant to give Playboy the opportunity to reject her. The employment counselor was adamant. Finally, Bobbie decided to give it a try.

At Playboy, she was well liked from the beginning. She was young, fresh-faced, and very pretty. Bobbie started at $70 a week in September 1960, as a "floater," an attractive girl assigned to no particular desk or person. Often she ended up stationed on the fourth floor of the magazine office at 232 E. Ohio Street, the slight, sexy-looking guardian of the editorial sanctum. But Bobbie was still uncertain about this job, which gave her pangs of insecurity. There was at least one reason she could put her finger on: Cynthia Maddox, who was the receptionist on the first floor.

Cynthia Maddox was a beauty. She had been a beauty at Lakeview High School. She was a beauty when she went to work for Playboy—before Bobbie did—as a combination receptionist, model, bunny, and company promotion gimmick girl. Bobbie Arnstein took a job that would present her with a daily reminder of what she considered to be her own deficiencies. She even took a small apartment on Dearborn Street with Cynthia. Bobbie's way of coping with a jealousy she couldn't rationalize was to confront it, to accompany it, to live with it, to try and conquer it. Bobbie wanted to get it right.

"Of course we were all in awe of her beauty," Bobbie's mother remembers. Cynthia and Bobbie would come to dinner at the Arnsteins' on Friday nights when they were first living together. Sometimes the girls would sun themselves behind the building where Bobbie's family lived.

"Even I watched that figure. We had an old apartment with a long hallway, and Cynthia would walk from the kitchen down to the living room, and I'd watch. She'd come over sometimes, and in those days the girls didn't wear bikinis much, but Cynthia wore a bikini, and they'd go down to the backyard to sit to sun themselves, and I used to say, 'Cynthia, if you're going to wear that here, everybody in the neighborhood is going to be over here.' And I used to watch her go down the hall. Even I used to watch her. I never saw such a figure. The most gorgeous figure that girl had. Bobbie used to say, 'She's so pretty. She's so much prettier than I am.' "

Hefner was working at breakneck speed then. His girly picture book was becoming a literary forum. Plans for book projects, real estate acquisitions, other magazines claimed his time. The Playboy Philosophy—one of the few philosophies without a death clause—was born then. Hefner, always at the center of the operation, seldom slept and never went home. Hefner made his office on the fourth floor his living quarters.

The sheer proximity of a bright, attractive woman in his outer office eventually commanded Hefner's attention. Bobbie was, for a short time, a social companion. Hefner describes it as having dated some. Bobbie would later give a more specific explanation of what she considered a very temporary physical liaison. Everybody at Playboy knew what Hefner meant when he talked about dates.

• • •

The money was pouring in. It was like some wild fantasy, a great modern capitalist adventure, the way *Playboy* magazine grew. Hefner and his burgeoning staff surged ahead, and Bobbie was along for the ride. Some months after she started, Hefner bought a big brick house at 1340 N. State, not far from the headquarters of John Cardinal Cody, then ranking official of the Archdiocese of Chicago with one of the largest concentrations of Roman Catholics in the world. The original idea of the house was for Hefner to get away from the office once in a while. Like most of the ideas he was having at that time, it worked out better than he expected. Now, instead of living in the office where he worked, he was working in the mansion where he lived.

Bobbie had acquired a mentor by then. Bobbie's friend Nancy was Hefner's private secretary. "She's so smart," Bobbie told her mother. "Nancy knows everything." Nancy knew she did not want to work at the mansion, anyway. When the inevitable summons came, Nancy opted to stay at the office. She sent the next best person, though. Bobbie Arnstein became Hefner's social secretary in 1962.

Soon afterward, Cynthia Maddox and Bobbie Arnstein moved in with Hefner. Hefner was never secretive about the fact that he liked pretty girls around, but he was also a benevolent provider who could be generous to a fault. At the time, Hefner was a notorious soft touch, who always seemed to be supporting a retinue of "artists" and sycophants who were down on their luck. Cynthia and Bobbie's subsidized apartment in the house was just down the hall from Bobbie's office. After a short time, she had the place to herself. Cynthia Maddox became ensconced as Hefner's main girlfriend; she would hold the title for about four years. Playboy was often being described as the "Playboy Empire." The house was hectic with parties and filled with celebrities of the moment and people on the Playboy payroll.

Hefner, who spent most of his time cross-legged on the famous round bed with a fur cover, talking on the telephone or looking at page proofs, was fighting a battle with the clock. Large amounts of money were now at stake, but he was not good at delegating authority and ended up making all the decisions himself. His quarters looked more like a data processing center than a bedroom. And Bobbie Arnstein's occupation was increasingly occupying.

Bobbie found herself screening requests, responding to emergencies, holding temperamental hands, digging up interesting monopoly partners when Hef fancied a game at an odd hour. If a financial disaster could be averted by Bobbie's ability to get an answer from Hef, she would sit with him until he was ready to talk. She was a tireless diplomat. There were times, her friends recall, when she was pitifully exhausted and disorganized, but she always broke the tape at the right time. Bobbie Arnstein was Hugh Hefner's umbilical cord to a business that had grown to be bigger than he was.

Enter Dick Rosenzweig, a dynamic businessman who had been moving steadily upward for six years. As a fledgling, he sold ads for *Playboy* and the short-lived *Show Business Illustrated*. He was made assistant to the promotion director, Victor Lownes, and later worked in the editorial section as director of special projects and book projects, then in syndication and production of *Playboy after Dark*. A suggestion made its way up the ranks, across Bobbie Arnstein's desk, that the post of executive assistant to Hefner be created. Rosenzweig got the job and established an office in the mansion in October 1963.

It never occurred to anybody that Bobbie Arnstein might be (and probably was, in fact) capable of doing part of the job Rosenzweig had been transplanted for. But it was the Golden Age of Playboy, and there was plenty of room at the top. Bobbie was queen of the hippest high society Chicago had ever known. The quite likable Rosenzweig became her ally and friend. Bobbie shrugged it off, figuring she couldn't handle his work even if Hefner had accepted her in Rosenzweig's place.

"She could have done my job a hell of a lot better than she thought she could," Rosenzweig said. Bobbie had a corner on the market as far as being a capable assistant to Hefner, but she considered herself incapable of doing anything else. The low opinion Bobbie Arnstein had of herself became apparent to the people around her. Feeling that she was at the pinnacle of what would be her career at Playboy didn't help. Constantly comparing her own body to the thousands of pictures of naked women that crossed her desk on their way to Hefner's quarters didn't help either. But Bobbie Arnstein was never too nuts about Bobbie Arnstein.

• • •

Bobbie and Eddie Arnstein were without a doubt the most adorable children on Kedzie Boulevard. All of the Arnsteins' neighbors in Logan Square knew the twins—a true distinction for their mother Evelyn—and the pair were doted on by a throng of loving family members and friends. To add to their cuteness, Bobbie and Eddie spoke with a German accent, thanks to the superior coaching of a *fraulein* hired to help around the house. "I'm twersty. I vant vater," they would say in their biggest, two-year-old voices. "They couldn't say 'cat' and 'rat' and 'bat,' " their mother remembers. "They used to say 'cot' and 'rot' and 'bot,' and one day Bobbie said to Eddie, 'I could say "cat." ' She told Eddie, 'You say "cat," ' and he kept saying 'cot.' After about three or four times at this he got disgusted and said, 'Well I could say "pussy." ' I never forgot that little thing, it was so cute."

Evelyn and Alvin Arnstein's first child, a son, Donald, was born in 1930. They lost a baby girl before the twins were born ten years later. Bobbie's father, who was by then heading up a lucrative dental practice, was delighted by (and partial to) his new daughter.

During their childhood, the twins spent every summer in the country (first at Hudson Lake, later in South Haven) with their mother and weekend father and every school year at Darwin Grammar School. They took elocution lessons when they were five. It kept the pair in popular demand. The South Haven kids held shows for their folks. Bashful Eddie would shy away from the microphone. His more aggressive sister would pull him by the ear, forcing his mouth against the instrument. "Now talk!" she ordered.

Bobbie was earmarked to be a regular Jewish American Princess. She danced. "You know, she'd get up and do bumps and grinds and things. Where she learned this, I don't really know," her mother said. By the time she was five, Bobbie had taken a year of ballet and was enrolled in modeling school.

When Bobbie and Eddie were ten, their forty-nine-year-old father died of a cerebral hemorrhage. Though he had been warned about high blood pressure, Dr. Arnstein had remained active. "They were very emotional children. Whether they had always been emotional and this was just the climax that brought it out of them, I don't know." The twins took it very hard. They seemed to withdraw.

●   ●   ●

Shirley Hillman, a pretty brunette in her mid-thirties who worked briefly at Playboy and affects a slight British accent, was Bobbie's best friend at the time of her death. She said that Bobbie maintained that she did not remember her father because she had been so young at the time he died. But Shirley never believed her.

The twins were very close and interdependent. Eddie would stand up in class and ask, "Bobbie, where's this?"·"Bobbie, how do you do that?" They finally had to be separated in school. After Dr. Arnstein's death, Eddie's grades began to fall and Bobbie began to emerge as the stronger of the pair, at least academically. "No, I can't do that. I can't leave my brother," was Bobbie's answer when her sixth grade teacher suggested that she skip a year. The principal called Mrs. Arnstein to school and explained that it wasn't fair to Bobbie or Eddie for her to remain behind. The children had a long talk, and Eddie urged Bobbie to go ahead. She did.

The money ran out a couple of years later. The Arnsteins moved into an apartment on Aldine with Evelyn's mother, sister, and brother-in-law. The relatives, plus a three-times-a-week maid, gave the kids a grand total of four mothers and very little male attention. Evelyn Arnstein said she later regretted the move.

When the time came Bobbie dated a lot. She went out with many of the boys nobody else would have—boys who were too short, boys who were nonathletic or not considered attractive—as long as they were "good company," she said. Adolescent whim got the better of Bobbie when she was a high school junior: she and her girlfriend, Denise York, spent an afternoon making each other's hair platinum blonde. Schoolmates were aghast.

During her senior year, two male teachers discreetly called Bobbie to the office. They confronted her with a picture appearing in the current *Playboy*; the girl looked exactly like Bobbie. "I tell you, I could not tell the difference," her mother said. The woman pictured had on a blue shirt with part of one breast exposed. The teachers didn't believe Bobbie's denial. They wanted an explanation. They wanted to know why she was taking her clothes off in public. Mrs.

Arnstein had to testify to Bobbie's innocence. There was an angry scene. Eddie kept that picture in his wallet for years afterward.

Bobbie began to retreat from her peripheral position in high school social circles. She was working part-time at a downtown shoe store and looking and acting different from people her own age. She didn't want to see anybody from Lakeview, much less go out with any of the boys from there. Instead, she dated men she met at work. The late-hour sessions during which Bobbie sat at the foot of her mother's bed and recounted her date that evening became more sporadic and less informative. High school graduation meant only relief, she said, like an escape from a bad dream.

Joining the labor force made Bobbie an official adult; moving away from the omnipresent grandmother, mother, and aunt was a further liberation. Though Bobbie's mother still considered theirs a close relationship, by the time Bobbie was working for Playboy, she was seeing her daughter less and less. When her mother warned that living and working in the same place could become a grind, Bobbie ignored the advice.

Hefner and his current sweetheart, the bunnies living in the house dormitory and whoever else happened to be a mansion fixture at the time became Bobbie's surrogate family. She would return home now and again, dragging a special boyfriend to meet the folks.

An eligible man had, in the meantine, walked into Evelyn Arnstein's life. Bobbie was getting pretty hot and heavy with Tom Lownes at about the same time her mother was managing the new romance. Evelyn was honeymooning in California when she learned that Bobbie had been in an auto accident.

●   ●   ●

Tom Lownes was in on the ground floor when *Show Business Illustrated* was launched by Playboy in April 1961. He was first named a contributing editor and was later imported from the *Miami Herald* as a full-time employee. With a little help from his brother Victor, Tom went on the payroll the day after Christmas. He met Bobbie Arnstein through the normal meshing of personal and professional relationships that characterized the way business was taken care of at Playboy. They began seeing each other regularly. Bobbie's mother got the idea that it was pretty serious when she saw Tom more than once for dinner.

Show Business Illustrated lasted only through April 1962; then Tom was named an associate editor of *Playboy*. Summer was ending for 1963 when Tom and Bobbie set out in a Volkswagen bound for Florida. It was a business-pleasure jaunt; Tom had an ex-wife and children to attend to.

Bobbie took over the driving in Kentucky. She hit a bump along the side of the highway, and the car veered off the road. Bobbie was thrown from the vehicle, but Tom remained trapped in the car. The Volkswagen flipped over and crushed him to death. Bobbie was rushed to a hospital in Louisville and treated for severe whiplash around her neck; some minor head, back, and leg injuries; and a broken arm. She was also treated by a psychiatrist during her four-day stay.

Bobbie was convinced that she had killed Tom. She repeated it over and over again, to her mother on the phone, to her older brother Don who flew to Kentucky with Cynthia Maddox to retrieve her, to anybody who would listen. The doctors were afraid that it would be dangerous for her to be alone, and Hefner insisted that Bobbie be brought back to the mansion to mend. He dispatched a limousine to meet the trio at the airport. Bobbie's convalescence crept along with somebody in attendance at all times. One afternoon Bobbie's aunt entered her niece's room and found Hefner, wearing blue pajamas, picking Bobbie up off the bed.

He turned and explained that Bobbie had been in a great deal of pain, that an ambulance was coming to take her to the hospital. Some people contend that the overwhelming guilt Bobbie felt after Tom's death ruined her life, that she was never quite the same after she was abandoned by her, as a friend put it, "one, true love." Bobbie was in and out of analysis from the time just before the accident until the day she died. But the people closest to her, people who had contact with her every day, argue that the accident was a blow to Bobbie's system that shook her up temporarily. She had not been maimed for life.

Lee Gottlieb, promotion director at Playboy, who was a senior editor at *Show Business Illustrated*, recalls Bobbie breaking down while dancing at a holiday party, saying, "This time last year Tom was here." He steered her off the floor and over to a cup of coffee. She calmed down twenty minutes later.

Bobbie was drinking too much. "She'd come into parties sort of weaving around," according to Gottlieb. Even Hefner noticed that she was overdoing the booze, though it never affected her work. He mentioned it to her. About a year after the car wreck, Bobbie gave up alcohol. The binges stopped as suddenly as they had started. Mary O'Connor, manager of the Playboy mansions, who was hired in the late sixties, said Bobbie found the taste of liquor intolerable. She once complained about a meal's entrée, cooked in sherry, saying it was "too winy." Marijuana became Bobbie's infrequent drug of choice.

There were no big romances after that, just men fading in once in a while. Bobbie would try people and discard them. "Something that would start out as a romance would end up in a friendship," Shirley Hillman says. "She considered herself a nonsexual being, so even though she would pretend the pose of sexuality, in the end she would be just downright herself. It's not usually the kind of thing that men find romantic about women, and she found all that kind of pose extremely phony. So her relationships would turn into a friendship rather than a passion. A pitter-pat, she used to call it."

• • •

Pitter-pat. Will you still love me tomorrow? It pained her that she couldn't play the game. She couldn't be coy, or hard to get, or pretend that there was somebody else, or refuse on the first date, or do any of those things women are supposed to do to sustain a male attention span. "Bobbie couldn't reconcile that pain with what she believed stupid. Women that did play that game—the pose and the making up to guys—she found pathetic. She hated it, but she knew it worked. So there she was in the middle of knowing what would work and then resenting people that did it and hating herself for ever doing it. She'd attempt it for a little while and then she'd say, 'Fuck it.' " That was her philosophy and method, says Shirley.

For a time, Bobbie flirted with homosexuality. "Intellectually, Bobbie could handle a woman loving another woman," Shirley says. Bobbie Arnstein and Shirley Hillman were in love. They were part of a generation of women discovering each other, who were learning that other women could be more than just competition to get men. An emotional solidarity was spreading. Bobbie and Shirley were such good friends that Shirley's husband, who had mysteriously gone blind about a year before Bobbie's death, resented the amount of time the two women spent together. They were so in love, Shirley explains, that they talked endlessly and daily. "I never thought that I could love anybody the way that I could Bobbie—more than I could love my children," Shirley says.

There were rumors that Bobbie and Shirley were lovers, though this was never true. Bobbie had tried lesbianism at one point, very early on, with a somewhat famous entertainer, but the idea of looking into another woman's eyes and saying, "Oh, darling," and kissing her just made Bobbie break up. So she never tried it again.

The subtle machismo that prevailed at Playboy was getting on Bobbie's nerves. By the late '60s Bobbie was avoiding men in the organization; she preferred the company of outsiders—a lawyer, a stockbroker, a newspaper columnist. "Her own social situation changed relative to me and the house in the last couple of years," says Hefner. "There was a raising of my own consciousness related to women's liberation and certain kinds of chauvinism that we've all been guilty of for years but not aware of. I indicated that if male executives could bring their girlfriends into the house for various social events—Sunday movies, etc.—there's no reason why she couldn't bring her boyfriends. But that wasn't until sometime in the '70s."

●　●　●

Years later, she would refer to it as her "fat period." By 1969, Bobbie was carrying almost 140 pounds on her five foot three frame, an acquisition roughly akin to contracting leprosy, especially in her line of work. But she loved food; the menus dished out at the mansion were fabulous, and her mother would augment them with occasional pastry. Browns, blues, blacks—she wore anything she thought would hide it. Bobbie's wardrobe seemed pretty blah when Shirley first encountered her. "She wore this two-piece navy blue outfit almost constantly. I used to think, 'My God, woman, don't you have anything else to wear?' "

Disgusted with herself, Bobbie checked into a Texas fat farm for a month—it was the first and only time she was away from Playboy for an extended period. "It was a place that had kind of a monastic quality about it," Hefner says. "Where you weren't able to talk to anybody. There were no telephones, no radio or TV, and you didn't talk to anybody else in the place for a solid month. It was primarily a water diet and a limited natural foods kind of thing. When she came back she was very high on natural foods stuff."

When Bobbie returned to Chicago in mid-1970 she had shed almost forty pounds, was neglecting her once-in-a-while cigarette, wouldn't touch liquor or dope, and got to be rather a pain in the ass to the kitchen about special foods that she wanted to eat. She looked great; she was "kicky," Mary O'Connor, who runs the Playboy mansion household, says. Her clothes were fun, even weird. Bobbie chucked her complete pre-fat farm wardrobe; it filled thirty cartons. She did frenzied shopping, picking up scads of three-inch platform shoes, denims, belts, feathers, scarves, chains, jewelry.

● ● ●

A mansion on the West Coast had become part of the Playboy properties and Hefner was spending more and more time there. Bobbie would shuttle back and forth. Wandering around in the Shangri-la atmosphere was an experience she seemed to relish. It was certainly something unique for a born and bred city girl noted for her hyperactivity. At thirty-plus Bobbie was taking up with men five and six years her junior. She made sarcastic remarks about young, hard bodies, but what she was really looking for was someone who would accept her honesty—men whose consciousnesses were malleable.

But all the exuberance and zealous approach to life that Hugh Hefner and others saw, her women friends say was a sham. Bobbie Arnstein may have made the decision to die by her own hand as early as 1970. Shirley says that Bobbie was deeply troubled by Sylvia Plath's bleak novel, *The Bell Jar.* The book, published in 1971, was the story of a young woman's failed attempts at love and her slide into a deep depression. Bobbie identified with Sylvia Plath; they were roughly the same age. She felt that her life was very painful. Even though she had been in analysis for a long time, she had been unable to find the answer, the key to what was making her so unhappy. Maybe it was because her mother was right—she would never be as beautiful as Cynthia Maddox. (The infatuation with Hefner over, Cynthia left Playboy, married a doctor, moved to the suburbs, had a couple of children, and was never heard from again.) Maybe Bobbie could blame the situation on her dead father, who left her. Maybe the villain was Hugh Hefner, who provided her with all the trappings of security without taking any emotional responsibility for her and who always seemed to be waiting for the right guy to come along and protect Bobbie.

After a while, Shirley Hillman maintains, even Bobbie was convinced that she should be a traditional woman who could love men despite their weaknesses, a woman who desperately wanted children, a woman who could depend on others, a woman who would welcome a subordinate role, who could learn to work with limitations. But Bobbie Arnstein was not that person. And she hated her inability to function in an imperfect role in a less than ideal world. She hated who she was not as much as she hated who she was.

• • •

Bobbie met Ron Scharf in a dress shop in the summer of 1971. He was about seven years younger than she, a part-time street dealer with what Bobbie called "beautiful, sensitive hands." Bobbie was very fond of Ron.

Shirley and Dick Hillman were then in Florida, but Bobbie spoke to them daily. She told Shirley about this great guy she'd met, how they had been seeing each other in the past few weeks, how he wanted her to go to Florida for a weekend. Testimony at a later court trial suggests that Ron went to Florida during the week prior to his trip with Bobbie. He made a deal with George Matthews for six and a half pounds of cocaine, but he didn't have any money. He promised to return on the weekend; when he did, he brought Bobbie along. According to Shirley, Bobbie may not have even known the purpose of Ron's trip. According to George Matthews's testimony two and a half years after the fact, Bobbie stuffed the cocaine in her purse and presumably carried it back to Chicago. That was September 1971.

Matthews was being watched by federal agents. Wiretaps were placed on a phone where Ron Scharf was living part of the time with Ira Sapstein (the other part of the time Ron was living with Bobbie in her apartment in the mansion). The conversations implied that Bobbie had buyers for the cocaine, though she later confessed to friends that she would have said anything in order to hang on to Ron. He was already showing a conjugal interest in another girl. In November of that year Ron sold some coke to a federal informant. An indictment was handed down, and Bobbie's name was not on it. Bobbie was brought in for questioning but made it clear that she would not cooperate. She and Ron continued to see each other.

• • •

Her wheels were spinning. Bobbie was beginning to feel like a closeted beast. With Hefner spending at least half his time in

California, Bobbie felt more and more useless. She revived the old idea of taking another job at Playboy, maybe an editorial job. Rosenzweig pointed out that her salary was a problem, that she was making way too much to go in as a trainee for a magazine job. He suggested that she buy some property, get out of the house, her womb, her jail. She and Mary O'Connor talked about starting a "country inn"—Mary already had a restaurant business on the side. None of the plans took hold. Bobbie became obsessed with her job problems.

One night, she retreated to her apartment, a sort of campy black, dingy alcove at the back of the building, and took a dosage of barbiturates (drugs she regularly used to sleep) that she was sure was large enough to kill her. Bobbie called Shirley to talk, even though it was already quite late. Shirley could tell by the way Bobbie was slurring her words that she had finally done the thing they had talked about several times. Bobbie didn't want to be saved; she had told Shirley that over and over again. But Shirley couldn't just let her die, either. She called the staff at the mansion. Bobbie was taken to nearby Henrotin Hospital, where her stomach was pumped. She was angry with Shirley. "I thought our friendship was beyond this," she said. Shirley replied that if Bobbie really wanted to kill herself she shouldn't have called.

Bobbie went through the motions of starting over. She made plans to move into another apartment inside the mansion. This room would be decorated in white, with green plants all around, a hammock, a bamboo swinging chair—what Mary O'Connor called "a lot of life." Her office was repainted white, in the same optimistic vein. Playboy changed Bobbie's title to "Assistant to the President," though her name did not appear on the magazine's masthead. She was given a raise. Most people thought she was doing a remarkable job of coming out of it. Even Shirley allowed herself to breathe a brief sigh of relief. She would say later, however, that in her heart, she knew that Bobbie was living on borrowed time.

The Ron Scharf drug case had gotten more complicated. Matthews fled. And, the Playboy people contend, Washington woke up to the fact that Bobbie Arnstein, associate of Hugh Hefner, might be indictable. Douglas Roller, a prosecutor out of the Washington office of the Department of Justice, was put on the case. Federal agents finally caught up with Matthews. They had plenty of evidence against the known drug trafficker. It wasn't his first offense.

Matthews turned state's evidence after he was promised a lighter sentence. He implicated Bobbie in a conspiracy to distribute cocaine. A new indictment was brought down on March 21, 1974. This time Bobbie Arnstein was at the head of the list. She was arrested that day carrying a small quantity of cocaine in her purse. One mansion insider said that Bobbie may not have used cocaine, but she always knew how to get it.

"It came as no surprise to me that she used cocaine," Hefner says. "But I didn't know that she used cocaine. What I'm saying is she didn't use it in my presence, and that's not a surprise. She would know that I would not be happy with it, and therefore she wouldn't do it. Unrelated to drugs, that's another form of saying that the nature of our relationship—that she wanted my respect—built up kind of a reserve."

Shirley urged Bobbie to take the stand in her own defense, to say anything she had to say to get off. Bobbie refused; she wouldn't implicate anyone, especially not Ron. For a while, Bobbie was confident that justice would prevail, that she wouldn't be convicted because she wasn't guilty. The headlines her arrest merited grated on her. Though she was one of a handful of defendants, she was the one who made the news; it was her picture that ran with the stories.

Bobbie felt a lot of preindictment and pretrial pressure. Convinced that they were trying to get Hefner behind bars using something she had to say, Bobbie refused to say anything. She didn't really know anything they wanted to hear anyway. After a few months the prosecutor's office believed her. Word was parceled down to Bobbie that Hefner was standing behind her. He contacted her himself. He paid her legal fees. Rosenzweig reassured her. Marilyn Cole, a mutual friend of Hefner and Bobbie, phoned her from London to reiterate the fact that her friends were still with her.

But Bobbie knew that Hefner was having difficulty coping with his own lawyers, who were pressuring him to disassociate himself from her. Bobbie was called to the prosecutor's office. U.S. Attorney Jim Thompson told her that her life might be in danger. He said several good sources had indicated to him that there might be a "contract," and Bobbie should trust neither friend nor foe. Clearly the idea was Bobbie should place no faith in Hefner, who, whether he knew it or not, had become something of a father figure to Bobbie. She refused protection.

Bobbie told Shirley that she would do herself in before anybody else got the chance. And she made good her promise by attempting suicide again. Same method, new apartment. Again she called Shirley. This time her friend was afraid of the publicity if she arrived at a Chicago hospital with drugged Bobbie in tow. She contacted a doctor-friend in Waukegan and drove Bobbie to Wisconsin for treatment.

The eight-week trial began. The prosecution's case was based mainly on the wiretap and the testimony of George Matthews (Bobbie specified in her suicide note that Matthews perjured himself.) Bobbie depended mostly on character witnesses. She again declined to go on the stand. If she testified, she knew she would have to face cross-examination, something she felt she would be unable psychologically to handle.

Ira Sapstein, named on the original indictment but not in the second indictment, resurfaced. In a meeting with his lawyer and the federal lawyers, he was evasive. The defense thought he might be able to clear Bobbie. The prosecution thought he was trying to cooperate enough to save himself from future indictment. The judge decided it was a lot of legal nonsense and threw the matter out of court.

Bobbie was found guilty in the conspiracy. The jury believed that she brought the cocaine from Florida to Chicago. The trial also established that she was a social user. On November 26, Bobbie got a conditional sentence of fifteen years in prison, subject to review (and a probable reduction) after ninety days of psychiatric tests. Bobbie's lawyers had chosen to go for the psychiatric test sentence because they believed there was no hope that they would get probation, even though the probation officer was sympathetic to Bobbie.

●   ●   ●

Hefner urged her to come out to California, as he had several times during the previous months. Her case was pending appeal. In December the *Chicago Tribune* ran a front page story calling Hefner the target in a drug probe by the Federal Drug Enforcement Administration. The inquiry was centered around drug use in both mansions. The DEA was also reopening the death of Adrienne Pollack, a Chicago bunny (whom Hefner claims he never even met) who died of an overdose in September 1973. Bobbie held herself responsible for everything.

Subpoenas were issued the following week for Hefner, Bobbie, Ron Scharf, and Mary O'Connor, among others. Bobbie couldn't see the end of the legal hassles. She feared she might be given the choice of immunity over a jail sentence. In that case, she would have to take the jail sentence, and, she told her friends, she would never go to jail.

Shirley tried to involve Bobbie in plans to start a new life on the West Coast. Over Christmas Shirley went to California and looked for an apartment where she, Dick, and the children could live with Bobbie. Marilyn Cole, tired of London, made plans to join them in their new home. Rosenzweig reminded Bobbie that the staff was sorely lacking her golden touch. Not only did Playboy want to get her out of Chicago for her own good, he insisted, they genuinely needed her.

But things didn't seem to be working. Bobbie couldn't live in the California mansion. She would have to take a hotel room until Shirley could join her. She would have to commute, and she didn't drive. She'd have to work regular business hours and leave at 7:00 because Hefner's lawyers didn't want her around. She was worried that this was the organization's way of gently easing her out.

She wasn't anxious to face Hefner, whom she hadn't seen since before the trial. In her darkest moments it crossed her mind that he wanted her out there only because he wanted Marilyn Cole out there. Bobbie knew that it would probably blow over, that it wasn't as bad as all that—intellectually. In her heart, it was pretty bleak. "She really thought it would change," Shirley says. So Bobbie decided to go ahead and move. She was in love with the house and grounds in California, and Playboy was too much a part of her life not to give it a second chance.

The Sunday before she was scheduled to leave for the West Coast, Bobbie went over to Shirley and Dick's north side apartment for dinner. They shared a pizza and talked about parties. "In a large group Bobbie would move around from this person to that person to that person and carry on three conversations at once. We were talking about how Shirley acted differently. How she would concentrate on just one person," Dick says. At about eleven o'clock, a stockbroker friend and ex-boyfriend picked Bobbie up. They stopped and had coffee with some people he knew. Then, at about 1:00 A.M., he dropped Bobbie off at the mansion.

On her way to her apartment Bobbie stopped and asked a night houseman for a fifth of some kind of liquor. He said that he had to go get the key for the cabinet and added, "Are you taking it to a party or something, Miss Arnstein?"

Bobbie shook her head and smiled. "No, I'd just like to see what it feels like to have a hangover." She retreated to her little white apartment and roughed out a suicide note. She wanted to get it right, to set the record straight. ". . . Hugh M. Hefner is—though few will ever really realize it—a staunchly upright, rigorously moral man—and I know him well, and he has never been involved in the criminal activity which is being attributed to him now. That is the irony—but I have come to know that innocence is of small significance when compared to the real purpose and intent of the various government agencies engaged in pursuing him and leveling their harassment against me to the masses."

No one saw Bobbie leave the mansion at about 2:30 in the morning. She checked into the Maryland Hotel about half a mile away. She registered under the name Roberta Hillman, insuring the fact that Shirley would be unable to find her.

Bobbie didn't take any booze with her; she had enough pills in her handbag to kill her five times. She called Shirley, presumably after she had taken the pills and before she finished the final draft of her letter. Dick told her that Shirley was asleep, should he wake her up? Bobbie said no, that she would talk to Shirley in the morning.

When they found Bobbie's body she had been dead for about twelve hours. Nobody who knew her was surprised. Some friends got angry at Hefner, claiming if she hadn't had to go to California she might not have done it. Others pointed their fingers at the police. Shirley screamed, hid under the blankets, and shook. She knew "Bobbie killed Bobbie."

• • •

Bobbie wanted to be cremated, but good old social norms interfered again. Her mother arranged a Jewish service with an open casket. "I knew it would be a circus," Shirley said; that's why she declined to go. "If I had been a stronger person, I could have been with her and let her do it and comforted her at the time. I wish we could have gone off somewhere together and I could have been with her as long as she was determined to do this thing."

When Hefner heard that Bobbie was dead, he wanted to talk about it—to anybody who would listen. He made the decision to hold the press conference almost immediately. At the last minute Bobbie's mother asked him to be a pallbearer.

It was the first funeral Hugh Hefner remembers attending. "I don't remember having gone to any other funeral because no close friend had ever died," Hefner said. "I wanted to reach over and wake her up."

● ● ●

Shortly after Bobbie Arnstein's suicide, I went to the mansion to interview Hugh Hefner for this story. It was about seven o'clock on a chilly night. Lee Gottlieb and a security guard answered the door and led me to a conference room. Hugh Hefner sat across from me at a long wooden table and reminisced about Bobbie for over an hour. At one point, he leaned back and grabbed a Pepsi from a small portable refrigerator. Though we had a sad conversation about a terrible tragedy, I could see why Bobbie Arnstein had been fond of this kind and childlike man. Afterward, he showed me around the house. The police had sealed off Bobbie's apartment, but we went through her office and climbed the nearby spiral staircase up to Hefner's room. After the tour, Lee Gottlieb and I had a cup of coffee in the kitchen and talked about Bobbie for a while. A group of men were sitting in front of a television set in the main room as we crossed from the kitchen to the front door. Sonny and Cher were exchanging their usual banter, the standard opening of their variety show. We stood and watched for a few minutes.

When I looked around I saw Hefner sitting at a small table about ten feet away. He was going through newspaper clippings about Bobbie and the press conference, trimming the corners and pasting them in a scrapbook. He was wholly absorbed in the task.

In the fall, the U.S. Attorney's office, under the direction of Sam Skinner—Jim Thompson was trying to get the Republican nomination for governor—sent a long memo to the Justice Department in Washington detailing the information they had about Hefner. The grand jury had already quit hearing evidence in the matter, and the investigator assigned to the case had been transferred out of town. Washington did not respond to the memo. Sam Skinner told the *Chicago Tribune* that the charges against Hefner did not stand up and that "the people who made them were misinformed."

He added, "It is a dead issue."

Hugh Hefner did not comment. It was the day before New Year's Eve; the investigation had gone on fifteen months. I thought about

Hefner clipping the final installment out of the paper, pasting it in the book, and closing the book forever.

• • •

Hugh Hefner returned to the house in Beverly Hills and never really lived in Chicago again. Before the year was out, Mary O'Connor was in California, managing the West Coast mansion. Christie Hefner joined the Playboy staff. It was soon common knowledge that her father was grooming her for an important job at the company—eventually she would become president of the organization. Christie Hefner was of the opinion that Los Angeles was a lousy place for a young single woman to live. She felt the same way about the State Street mansion and lived there only a short time before moving to her own apartment. The lavish parties ended abruptly now that Hefner was gone. The mansion was closed temporarily at first, then finally for good. The house was put up for sale.

The company would suffer a number of setbacks during the next five years. A few very close associates of Hefner's were transferred to Los Angeles, but most of the old group left during at least two instances of massive staff cuts. (Lee Gottlieb went to another job. Dick Rosenzweig went to California.) Playboy lost its gambling license in Atlantic City, and that hugely profitable club had to be sold. Hefner built a new society on the West Coast, but it was not quite the same.

• • •

In August 1984, Playboy donated the mansion to the Art Institute of Chicago. Christie Hefner made the announcement at a press conference. The mansion has been renamed Hefner Hall.

3

Tainted Tylenol

When seven people with no connection to one another poisoned themselves with cyanide-laced capsules of Extra-Strength Tylenol in September 1982, I thought the Chicago-area setting appropriate. The killer had been extremely bold on the one hand but also completely cowardly. The resulting deaths were senseless, though the crime was incredibly calculated.

I have been told that, although the authorities are 99-percent certain they know who tampered with the drugs, the chance of a legal solution to the murders being found is pretty remote.

A couple of things struck me about the Tylenol case. Though most of the victims lived in the suburbs—Paula Prince, an airline stewardess found dead in her Old Town apartment, was the only Chicagoan—the two main suspects in the case frequented the same lakefront neighborhood. Both suspects considered themselves outlaws, romantic figures who lived apart from society by choice, too smart or too crazy to make lasting connections.

Several years ago Roger Arnold would have looked fairly typical of the guys hanging around the Lincoln Park saloons, particularly among the afternoon and early evening crowd. He was forty-eight years old, about five feet eight inches tall, with a physique that looked strong but not intimidating. Roger Arnold always dressed in the same clothes: a denim jacket and pants and a worn denim cap with a union button pinned to the top. His beard and moustache looked as though he had just decided to grow them a couple of weeks earlier. His aviator-style glasses had dark frames with tinted lenses. Had he worn fingerless gloves, you would have expected him to get off a motorcycle. As it was, he drove a beater, a 1978 Chevy that looked older.

North Avenue had changed since Paul Tyner's heydey, and the tradesmen—the carpenters, the electricians, and the pipe fitters, who ate lunch at Sonny's, a tavern and grill midway between O'Rourke's (which had moved to the south side of North Avenue) and the Old Town Ale House—wore work clothes: jeans, flannel shirts, and new-looking polyester caps with company insignias. The young Old Town professionals wore cotton, linen, and twill when it was warm and corduroy as the weather changed. The number of people dressed like Arnold had diminished considerably, until the middle-aged laborer who had been loading and unloading trucks at the Jewel warehouse in Melrose Park for many years stood out against the Old Town landscape. His personal style labeled him a freak, no longer a popular person to be. Roger Arnold was oddly archaic, a man unaware that his time had passed.

The feeling of anonymity that he got in the north side bars was an old habit. Arnold had been drinking there for a few months this stretch, though he had come off and on for short periods for his whole life. He had started drinking in these places when he dropped out of high school and lived near Halsted and Fullerton, when he was just a kid. It was an occasional thing. He would stop at O'Rourke's in the early evening after work, sit quietly by himself at the end of the bar, and drink several tall screwdrivers before he returned to his apartment in an old Italian section of the near south side. Sometimes he would go down to the Ale House or to Lincoln Avenue, a few blocks north, to Sterch's or the Oxford Pub. It didn't make much difference; it was mostly the same people, anyway. He had a few acquaintances in the bars, the way bar people do.* There was a girl he talked to sometimes and Ron Rossetti, a dark-haired young guy who edited a sports magazine. But basically, he didn't trust other people; they were noisy, and he kept to himself.

• • •

Gus Stevens, the proprieter of Sterch's, a small bar and grill on Lincoln Avenue that was usually crowded with sports fans and their girlfriends, was probably one of the most beloved guys in Lincoln Park. Gus was almost forty, but he could pass for much younger. He looked and acted like a teddy bear. Like many of the local tavern owners, he had a small group of regulars who drank at his place in the early evening—they were people who liked to talk to him and play pinball and rock 'n' roll on the jukebox.

The afternoon that Roger Arnold happened into Sterch's was pretty ordinary, and nobody paid much attention to him. A lady friend of his came in, they started talking, and the tavern began to grow crowded as it got later. Mike Meyer, a thirty-six-year-old one-

---

*All of the people in this story are real. The names of most have been changed and the locations mixed up to disguise and protect them.

time public schoolteacher who liked to hang around Sterch's, get drunk, be morose and occasionally belligerent, ended up sitting next to Arnold and his girl. Baby-faced Meyer, with a moustache and curly red hair, made an insulting remark to Arnold's girlfriend. Arnold turned to Meyer, said, "Get out of my face, asshole," and thought that would be the end of it. But the younger man was drunk enough to continue his attempt to talk to the woman. Roger Arnold pulled a gun. When Gus told him to put it away and get out of the bar, he pointed the gun at Gus. Gus moved to call the police, and Arnold put the gun away and left. Later that evening, Stevens filed a formal complaint against Arnold, and a warrant was issued for his arrest.

When Arnold stopped by O'Rourke's a few days later, Al Kendall, the bartender, knew he was the guy who had pulled the gun at Sterch's. In fact, almost everybody who tended or owned a bar along North and Lincoln avenues knew about Roger Arnold. A number of the regulars had heard the talk, and they had been busy remembering old encounters with the guy. Chuck Cameron, a sixty-five-year-old cab driver and spontaneous speech maker, and Bruce Lyman, a somewhat younger golf hustler, who had both been around the Ale House for twenty years, had been watching the pope on the saloon television when he was in Chicago in the fall of 1979. To the amusement of the other customers, Cameron and Lyman were having an argument about the degree to which Pope John Paul II offended them. The two finally agreed that the pope should be assassinated, often their sodden conclusion as to what to do with a television celebrity they couldn't stand. But then another argument erupted when Cameron suggested that the pope should be disposed of with a hand grenade and Lyman wanted to do the pontiff in by more conventional means. Roger Arnold had entered the conversation at this point, they remembered, saying that plastic explosives were without a doubt the most effective way of getting rid of somebody but, if you were going to shoot instead, it would be a critical error to use anything but cyanide-tipped bullets.

Fred Schnell—who committed suicide himself a few months after the Tylenol murders—recalled another incident with Arnold. He had been in the Ale House in an animated discussion with another patron about whether or not one could beat a lie detector test. Schnell's companion said he knew a doctor who said you could take a drug and, with coaching, beat the test. He couldn't remember the name of the drug. At this point, Arnold supposedly entered the conversation and insisted that Schnell's friend call his doctor. The doctor said that 30 milligrams of Librium would skew the test.

Of course, neither of the incidents really meant anything. But now that Roger Arnold had pulled a gun, the regulars thought that he might be a little too volatile. He might even be a little crazy.

Not that a guy who was armed was a new thing in the taverns of Old Town. Al knew that at any given moment almost half of the men in the bar were carrying a weapon. But having a concealed weapon was one thing; pulling it out was another. Not only was it possible that a gun-toting patron would hurt somebody; he also might cause some other maniac to pull his gun.

When Arnold came into O'Rourke's the next Friday, Al's eyes narrowed, and he clenched his teeth around the end of the Pall Mall he was smoking. Arnold took a seat at the rear corner of the bar, as was his custom. Kendall grasped the end of his cigarette between his thumb and index finger, threw it down on the floor in front of him between the cash register and the bar, and crushed it out with his foot. He made Arnold a tall screwdriver. One thing he knew about Roger Arnold: drinking didn't have much effect on his behavior one way or the other. Al had never seen him drunk, or even drinking with purpose, and this evening was no different.

Arnold sipped at the drink for half an hour before he began talking with Ron Rossetti. Rossetti had also heard about the incident at Sterch's, and he mentioned it to Arnold right away. Arnold explained what had happened and how he felt that he had had no choice but to do what he did. The discussion drifted to Arnold's personal life; most of it Rossetti had heard before. Arnold told how he had recently gotten divorced from his wife Delores. They had been married for twelve years, she was a manic-depressive, she'd been bedridden for more than three years, and she'd been in and out of mental institutions the whole time he knew her. When they were divorced, he said, he kind of lost everything. His wife got the $48,000 home. Arnold got the Chevy and a little cash. It was funny, he told Rossetti, he had been in the joint for seven years, and he didn't think it could get much worse than that on the outside, but it had. A moment later, however, Arnold cheered up. He told Ron that he was looking forward to his annual vacation in the Far East. At least he'd get laid. He already had his tickets to Thailand, and he was set to leave Friday the 15th. Rossetti and Arnold shook hands when Arnold left.

Ron said something to Al across the bar that he didn't quite understand, so Al moved closer.

"You know that guy, don't you?" Rossetti asked. "Roger Arnold?"

"Yeah, I know about that guy," Kendall replied. "He pulled a gun on Meyer and Gus in Sterch's the other day."

"Who deserves it more than Meyer and Gus?"

It was almost comical listening to a guy like Rossetti talk about pulling guns on people. Rossetti acted like a little old lady or a pathetic wreck, depending on how much he had to drink. Sometimes Al thought he didn't even belong in a bar. When he said it was all right to put a gun in somebody's face in a bar, Al Kendall got angry.

"Listen, asshole," he snarled at Rossetti without raising his voice. "If somebody pulled a gun on you, you'd go fuckin' crazy. You'd have him arrested for assault immediately. You think that's funny, that somebody'd pull a gun in a bar?"

Rossetti backed down just as Al knew he would. "You've got to understand, the guy's got problems. He had a hard life. He was in the joint for seven years. His wife went crazy, and then she got everything in the divorce. . . ."

"I don't care about that. Just don't tell me it's OK to pull a fuckin' gun in a bar."

● ● ●

Maybe it was just that Roger Arnold made Al nervous now, or maybe it was the argument with Rossetti, but when Arnold came in the following week, Joe Gallagher was in O'Rourke's and Al told Joe the whole story. Even though Gallagher was in his late thirties, with his bright blue eyes and curly brown hair, he still looked like an Irish kid. He had graduated from the police academy a couple of years ago, and he just loved being a cop. Gallagher made a phone call, and inside of a few minutes two uniformed officers arrived in a patrol car and took Arnold outside. They frisked him, found the gun, lectured him, and sent him home. They didn't want to mess around with all the paperwork involved in an arrest, which was fine with Kendall. All Al Kendall wanted was never to see Roger Arnold again, and he figured that Arnold was the type of guy who wouldn't come back if he thought people were watching him.

Al was right about that. Arnold wouldn't come back. But Al Kendall saw him again.

Three days after Roger Arnold was frisked outside of O'Rourke's, seven people took Extra-Strength Tylenol capsules that had been filled with potassium cyanide, and they died.

Ten days later Arnold was arrested on an aggravated assault charge stemming from the incident in Sterch's, but the reason that Al saw him on the ten o'clock news was that Arnold was also being considered a leading suspect in the Tylenol murders.

For three days Arnold was in police custody. Police found cyanide, weapons, and a book on how to kill people in his apartment. He was released.

Eight months later, on Lincoln Avenue, Roger Arnold spotted John Stanisha, a man the police said Arnold mistook for Oxford Pub owner Marty Sinclair. Sinclair, Arnold thought, had given his name to the police in connection with the Tylenol case. Arnold shot Stanisha to death and was convicted of murder in January 1984.

Marty Sinclair closed his business and left town.

• • •

Five-forty-nine West Belden, just off Clark Street, was an anomaly in its Lincoln Park neighborhood. The sprawling forty-four unit brick complex set in a quiet residential block that had been designated a landmark in the '70s was still operated as a boardinghouse, despite the fact that the neighboring greystones had long ago been rehabbed into cooperatives and condominiums worth hundreds of thousands of dollars. The living quarters were set on four floors and were by no means uniform. Some of the apartments were self-contained, with two rooms and a bathroom; others were just a space with a bed and hallway access to a toilet, a shower, and a couple of pay phones. All of the apartments were furnished with dilapidated Danish modern chairs, cheap wooden tables, and tired carpeting of indeterminate color. Besides the transient young people who lived there—DePaul University students looking for a permanent situation, struggling artists and writers working in New Town bars and restaurants as waiters and cooks—there was a handful of middle-aged permanent residents, like the house painter who lived with his cats and played classical music all day. There were also some elderly people on fixed incomes who liked the close proximity of the small shopping center on the east side of Clark Street and the feeling that they were safe. Maybe it was because so much of the space was shared, or maybe it was due to the fact that nobody living at 549 had much money, but there was a good community feeling to the building; a kind of society had grown up there. Some of the inhabitants made friendships that endured long after they had gone on to bigger and better things.

Bob Richardson was thirty-four years old and socially prominent at the Belden boardinghouse. He had arrived there in the late summer of 1981, a tall, thin fellow with sandy brown hair, a beard and a moustache, and wire-rimmed glasses. He had established himself quickly as an intelligent, talkative character who loved gadgets and knew his way around bookkeeping ledgers and computer terminals.

Nancy Richardson was the antithesis of her husband. Some of the tenants thought she was spooky because she was so utterly silent. Her neighbors at the Belden heard her speak only a few sentences during the time she lived there, although her replies were articulate enough. Questions were seldom directed to Nancy, anyway. She was fat, dumpy, and pale, with straight brown hair. She wore glasses and dark clothing and did not look like she wanted to be approached. Most people attributed Nancy's nonentity status to her husband's aggressively extroverted, almost dominating ways and to the fact that she always seemed to be out working while her husband was always hanging around doing nothing.

The foyer at 549 Belden operated like an old-fashioned hotel lobby. There was a large wooden desk set on a tile floor and behind it an old painted grate with pigeonholes for the tenants' mail. Tom Kline, the twenty-five-year-old, fuzzy-haired building manager, would sound one of the buzzers to their rooms when somebody upstairs had a phone call. Bob Richardson used the hallway as his salon. When Nancy left for work (for a few months she worked at the Lakeside Travel Agency in Winnetka; later she took a job at an accounting firm downtown), Bob would go downstairs, leaving the door to their two-room, third-floor apartment open. He picked up the newspapers—the *Chicago Tribune* and the *Sun-Times*—at the drugstore on the corner a few steps away, sat down at the desk, and began reading. Though Bob appeared to have all the time in the world, he always looked like he had gotten dressed in a hurry. His clothes almost matched. They were muted plaids worn with understated patterns or the wrong color sports shirt. Most of his things seemed to have been handsome at one time, but now they were shabby. Sometimes he would wear a sport coat, also well made and threadbare. His outfits caused some people to characterize him as an absentminded professor, interested in books and reading and writing but not very concerned about his appearance. Bob Richardson was not absent-minded at all.

Most days, Bob would just sit there at the desk, bidding the other residents a good day and waiting for Tom Kline and his dog, Tigger, a big, mangy mutt who had been left tied to a door by an exiting tenant, to get up. Kline was a night owl, partly by choice, but partly because tenants always had problems that needed immediate atten-tion in the middle of the night. His afternoon chores consisted mainly of cleaning up after people who had just moved out. One of Kline's chronic complaints was that his place was a mess because he didn't feel like cleaning his own room after he had finally finished cleaning somebody else's room. Another chronic complaint he had was that the $150 a week he was paid—he also got a free apartment—wasn't enough for him to go to the racetrack as often as he liked.

Tom Kline thought Bob Richardson was very gutsy and very shrewd, especially when he told him about using aliases to collect tax refunds. Richardson had run his own tax business in Kansas City, he told Kline, and that was how he had learned to hide money and stage rip-offs.

Bob Richardson never talked in much detail about personal things, but he did occasionally mention that he and Nancy had had a little daughter, Toni Ann, who died when she was five years old of a congenital heart defect, seven years earlier. Nancy would never get pregnant again, he swore, because they wouldn't be able to take another tragedy like that. Tom used to kid him about it good-naturedly, telling him that they should adopt a kid. Bob told Tom that he was very sorry about what had happened but that life was what it was, and it went on.

Bob Richardson had a vindictive streak which Tom Kline said was understandable. He shared Bob's feeling that the system was designed for rich people, and he agreed that in theory the way to get back at people was by playing an angle, screwing up a credit rating, putting together a phony deal. But there was another side to Richardson, a kind of edginess that made Tom nervous. Richardson once told Kline a story about how cows are cut up with a chain saw and how a chain saw is used to rustle cattle. Even Kline thought this was strange stuff from his mild-mannered friend.

In March 1982, the travel agency where Nancy Richardson worked went out of business, and when she tried to cash her last paycheck it bounced. This infuriated Bob, and he promised that he would get

boxes. They left a forwarding address to the middle of nowhere in Amarillo, Texas.

• • •

Shortly after the cyanide deaths, Richardson sent a letter to Johnson & Johnson, makers of Tylenol, asking that $1 million be placed in a bank account belonging to his wife's former employer to "stop the killing." The authorities took a couple of days to figure out that Bob and Nancy Richardson, whose real names were James and LeAnn Lewis, were responsible for the extortion note, which was postmarked New York City. Two months after the Tylenol deaths, the Richardson-Lewises were picked up in Manhattan.

LeAnn was released, but her husband was eventually convicted of attempted extortion. He refused to take the stand in his own defense, but has always maintained that his sole motive was to focus attention on the boss who had written LeAnn the bad check. The police, for months afterward, continued to try to prove that James Lewis had returned to Chicago to plant the tainted Tylenol capsules. (There was some evidence that Lewis may have murdered Ray West, an elderly client of Lewis's income tax service, in Kansas City, Missouri, in 1978. He was released on a legal technicality in that case.) Lewis, also convicted of income tax evasion, has said he was very sorry about writing the letters; he expects to spend most of the rest of his life in jail.

No one knows what happened to LeAnn.

4

The Last Stand Of Roger Patten

This is a story about guns and violence, and death that comes randomly at twilight in a big city. But it is really a story about patterns and the control of poverty. Roger Patten could not change his life any more than he could save himself from an early death. A lifetime of poverty made this ending inevitable.

Money buys distance. Certainly distance from poverty, but also distance from despair, guns, violence, police, and the sudden death that comes with poverty. The distant city people try not to pay attention to what goes on among the less fortunate. They are legitimately afraid of being sucked into a pool of grief, anxiety, helplessness, and rage. The other side of empathy is a thing to be feared.

But the summer brings the territory into sharp relief. The city is on the street, and the street has taverns, multiunit rental buildings, criminals, truants, dope addicts, teenage welfare mothers, madmen, and storefront emporiums where people who cannot do anything else go to get work for the day.

Everyone in Chicago likes to go to the beach on Lake Michigan, which runs the length of the city. It is almost always a little cooler near the lake, and everyone is welcome. Young people gather in great crowds to see their friends. Adults just want to be out of doors. Old folks go to remember what the beach was like when they were young.

In June, when the sky does not go dark until eight or nine o'clock and summer is still new, the lakefront is alive with people who seem to have all the time in the world. The shore becomes a place of chance encounters, little celebrations of life, reckless euphoria, and spontaneous combustion. Water and sand can irritate as well as soothe.

• • •

The Patten family—all nine of them—grew up near this inland sea, and somehow they always managed to get along. Though each individual has expressed a desire at one time or another to pull up stakes and settle in a rural place where life is less frantic—in Wisconsin or California or Indiana—only one of the Pattens has succeeded in leaving town. George and Joan Patten are middle-aged, and they have lived north and south, usually in neighborhoods that were either on the way up or on the way down. "We're always one jump ahead of the wrecking ball," George Patten likes to say.

George is German-Irish, and his wife is of English extraction. They're Christians with a strong church affiliation, and they believe in trying to make ends meet and in being kind to their neighbors. They met in the Southtown Theater, were married at St. John the Baptist Church, and started a family in an apartment at 65th and Normal. Thirty years ago they had plans and dreams about the future, but they don't remember what they were. Whatever dreams they had are long gone; too many things got in the way.

There were children, seven of them, five boys and two girls, born between 1948 and 1961, and Joan had some health problems. George took to drinking and, while he usually held some kind of factory job, there was never enough money in it. Then George started having heart problems.

The family lived in cramped quarters and watched television, and as soon as they were old enough the kids started to make their own ways in the outside world. George and Joan abandoned their private aspirations in the face of the more immediate business of survival. They gave up finding a way out for themselves and instead hoped their children would find their own ways. Some of them would, and some would not. Their youngest, Roger, was one who didn't.

• • •

It happened at Oak Street Beach, an appropriate spot. At that point on the near north side, the beach is more a frame in which to pose than it is a playground. There isn't a great deal of sand; what there is instead is a huge cement walkway, a stone promenade, a showcase whose audience is the traffic buzzing down Lake Shore Drive and the condominium owners beyond, who view the L-shaped property from the highest-priced terraces in Chicago. Oak Street is a peculiar kind of crossroads. A couple of blocks south of the beach there's the Northwestern Memorial Hospital complex, with its special facilities for training doctors, nursing pregnant women, and treating crazies. Farther north is Lincoln Park, the Farm in the Zoo, and young adults on roller skates. Traveling due west, you get an entirely different feeling: you pass the Oak Tree restaurant, a well-known haven that's open twenty-four hours a day to actors and musicians, hookers and street types, and the police of the 18th district. A few blocks west, there's the Moody Bible Institute. And finally, after the fancy restaurants and the time-worn delicatessens, the designer outlets and the resale shops, the strollers, and the stalkers, there's the high-rise public housing project known as Cabrini-Green, a frightening and depressing warehouse full of humans.

The location of the Oak Street Beach makes it attractive to a varied clientele. Tourists who want to see the lake without straying too far from their Gold Coast hotels go to Oak Street, as do newspaper photographers who need a weather picture. Twilight comes a little earlier at this beach than elsewhere, because the sun doesn't have to sink very far before it is obscured by the tall buildings that surround the corner. Even when the days are long, the beach is dim and most of the people have gone home by 9:00 P.M., and the gentle sound of the water lapping against the shore is broken only occasionally by the scream of a siren.

Roger Patten made his last stand at the Oak Street Beach. Sometime after 8:30 P.M., on June 4, George Patten's youngest son caught a lifeguard's attention by waving around what appeared to be a gun. The eighteen-year-old was drunk and staggering, witnesses said, and he was making threats, though these were pretty incoherent. The lifeguard called the police. Four officers responded to the call, including Sergeant Hubert Heraty. When Roger was confronted by the police he refused to surrender. The four policemen surrounded him. By this time, Roger had the toy gun stuck into the waistband of his pants. "The indications are that what he had looked very much like a gun," says Robert Wooldridge, an administrator in the Police

Department's Office of Professional Standards. "The officers told him at least four times not to pull the gun from his waistband." As the police approached Roger, commanding him to drop his weapon, the boy drew a butcher knife from inside his pants leg and laid it on the ground. According to one witness, he now began to shout that they would never take him alive. The police told him not to move. They began to close in. Roger Patten moved. He reached for the model pistol stuck in his belt. According to First Deputy Police Superintendent Leonard Zaleski, the bullet that struck Roger in the right side of the back of his head was fired by Sergeant Heraty. The police loaded Patten's bleeding body into a nearby paddy wagon and carried him to Northwestern Hospital, where he was pronounced dead on arrival at about five minutes after nine o'clock.

Four days later, at the Birren Funeral Parlor on Wellington Avenue at Southport, the remains of Roger Patten were cremated. There had been a few mourners at the service the day before: seven members of the immediate family; a couple of people who work with Joan Patten at Grant Hospital; a friend of George Patten's—a guy he met when he was in the hospital after his first heart attack six years ago; a couple of kids Roger had known when he was growing up; several people from the building where Roger had lived with his sister Suzen and his brother Craig; and a woman named Helen, who was Roger's friend when he had the job of sweeping up the Treasure Island on Lawrence Avenue. At the service, Helen told George Patten she couldn't figure out why "one human being would want to do this to another human being." George Patten said he didn't understand it either. He didn't know why Roger had to get shot in the head, from behind, from five feet away. A minister from the Salvation Army gave the eulogy. After the funeral, Roger's sister took the small brown and white box containing Roger's ashes home to her apartment. Her father had told her he couldn't bear to have the box around. A life insurance policy paid $1,000 when Roger died. The cremation cost $900; it was all George and Joan Patten could afford.

●   ●   ●

It might have been different. If Roger Patten had been born into a family that was luckier and had fewer mouths to feed, the odds in favor of his growing up into a healthy adult and living to a ripe old age might have been greater. Things were not going well for the

Pattens when Roger arrived on February 19, 1961, and they only got worse. Roger's chances grew slimmer each year. The Pattens, living near North Avenue and Cleveland, had become Salvationists by the time he was born, and when Roger was five years old, his father says, he was "already beating the drum for the Salvation Army." He and his brothers David and Bobby and his sister Suzen became members of the Lakeview Corps at 5100 N. Pulaski. When Roger was old enough, he attended Camp Wonderland in the summer. The fee for camp was $20, but the Pattens didn't have enough money and the Salvation Army absorbed the cost.

The same year he started beating the drum, Roger was in a car accident. He was thrown into the air by the car that hit him, and he landed on top of it, on his head. "With young kids like that, their heads are like Jello," George Patten says. He was in Ravenswood Hospital for several weeks, and when he was released he had to sleep in a special bed and wear a protective contraption that looked like a football helmet. The physical damage healed, and no one gave a thought to possible psychological damage.

After the accident, Roger began to put on weight and keep to himself. Five years later, he was about fifty pounds overweight and introverted, and his schoolmates taunted him. He felt he was different; shy and easily embarrassed, he became a chronic absentee. As a sixth grader he weighed almost 240 pounds, even though he stood only about five feet tall. "I didn't know how big he got from one year to the next," his mother says. "Every time he got nervous he would eat." His sister walked him to the Stockton School at 44th and Beacon each day. Roger dreaded, even hated, school by then. The next year, one of his teachers referred to him as "a blimp" in front of his classmates. It was the last straw; Roger refused to go back to school. Suzen remembers several occasions when school authorities visited the house to try to make him return, but it was a difficult time for other members of the family, and there really wasn't anybody available to supervise Roger's activities.

Fourteen years separated Roger from his oldest brother, Craig. It had been some years since Craig had lived with his parents. Craig was good-looking, trim with dark hair, and could usually find someone to take care of him. For a while he was married, and for a while he had trouble with drugs. Even after he quit taking hard drugs, he continued to pop pills intermittently. Sherry, two years younger than Craig, had also married and started a family of her own. Even though she lived in Chicago, she was busy and began to lose touch with her folks. Older brother Carl had managed to get into the police academy and was going with a girl he planned to marry. Suzen had dropped out of high school in her third year and was still home, helping her mother recover from surgery for cancer. George Patten had suffered his first heart attack and lost his job at the American Decal Company on account of his precarious health. Roger's brother Robert had joined the Navy. David, who was three years younger than Robert and three years older than Roger and was frequently in trouble with the police, had been arrested for aggravated battery when Roger was about fourteen. David spent about a year in Cook County Jail, was eventually convicted, and was sent to the prison in Pontiac, Illinois, to serve his sentence. Soon afterward, Joan Patten went to work as an assistant dietitian at Grant Hospital, Suzen married and moved out, and Roger found himself alone at home a lot with his father. Roger and his parents lived in a few apartments in and around Uptown and during his early teens finally settled at 2657 W. Ainslie.

●   ●   ●

Teenagers often reach a stage at which it becomes impossible for them to communicate with their parents, and in that respect Roger was a lot like kids his age. But in other ways he was very different. When his peers went on to high school, Roger began taking odd jobs. A neighbor would hire him to paint or make minor repairs on a building. He fell into a routine. If the weather was bad or if she had an unusual number of bundles to carry, he would accompany his mother on the bus to work. He often met her at the hospital and saw to it that she got home from work safely. During the day he would clean up the house, washing the floors and the windows and taking the laundry out. When George Patten wasn't feeling well, Roger would make supper for him. After his first heart attack, George suffered angina on a semiregular basis. Every few months he would take to his bed for three or four or five days.

When Roger was about sixteen his father developed trouble with his lungs, and though he continued to smoke Chesterfields, George Patten managed for the most part to give up drinking. Roger took a job as a maintenance man at an apartment building near the Pattens' apartment on Ainslie. The pay was $130 a month, and, his mother says, he gave a lot of it to his parents. The money that he kept for himself he generally spent on presents for other people. He bought plants, pictures, vases, statues of Buddha, and knickknacks for the apartment. Both of his sisters had children, and he provided pull toys, rubber balls, and games for the kids. He took a job at the grocery store. He came in Saturday night to clean up and finished the chores on Sunday.

He was alone most of the time, even when he was working. He took his leisure at Montrose Beach, sitting on the shore and watching the water. His sister Suzen thought he was very lonely during this time; though they had been close when she was still living at home, they began to drift apart. She had her hands full with a troubled marriage and a baby. "He was always hanging with kids that were younger than he was because they didn't care about his fatness. As his friends got older and they began to notice girls and got to drinking age, they sort of dropped Roger," Suzen says. He was five feet seven inches tall and weighed about 290 pounds.

The older Roger Patten got, the more quiet and withdrawn he became. "I think he hated himself more than he hated anybody else," his mother says. "He would save and save to buy something, and then he would give it away to somebody else." She remembers walking down the street with Roger one day when he caught his own reflection in a plate glass window. The youngster with the light brown hair and delicate features turned to his mother with tears in his eyes and told her, "I look like three people." Because of his shyness and lack of education, some people thought that Roger was retarded. He had trouble getting jobs because he was unable to fill out a job application, and, because he vanished into his own world so much of the time, he had trouble keeping the jobs he did get.

After Robert got out of the Navy, he came back and lived with Roger and his parents for a short period. Carl was a policeman by then, and he had broken away from the family completely. Carl wanted nothing to do with people he considered losers; he was ashamed of his family, his father would say later; he had gotten away from the poverty and the drugs and the unemployment, and was making a new life in another part of town.

Roger felt bad about Carl's attitude; he knew how much it hurt his mother. And the day that Robert moved out of the apartment on Ainslie, that bad feeling turned to hatred. Robert had called Carl, who owned a station wagon, and asked him to help him move his things to a place in a small town in Indiana where he had taken a job. When Carl arrived, he refused to come upstairs. Roger carried a pile of Robert's things down to the car and greeted Carl. Carl refused to acknowledge Roger; he stared straight ahead and motioned toward the rear of the station wagon, indicating where Roger should set Robert's things. Roger went back up to the apartment, sat down in a chair, and began to cry.

• • •

No one remembers when Roger began collecting guns, but his sister recalls that she noticed this preoccupation a couple of years earlier. Roger had several life-size replicas of wartime weapons, and they were made of cast iron. Roger purchased the guns for his collection through ads in specialty magazines. At first, the artificial weapons stayed in a box in his room, as toys to look at, not to play with. Roger Patten's other hobby was reading. He carried books around with him.

Roger had a small library of dog-eared volumes of personal philosophy. He had several works by Hugh Prather; he read and reread *Notes to Myself: My Struggle to Become a Person* and *Notes on Love and Courage*. Both books outline Prather's point of view about life, death, being what you are, and living the way you live; they are treatises typical of the self-determination literature that preceded what Tom Wolfe would dub "the me-decade." *Notes to Myself* takes the form of confessional vignettes, lessons that helped the author toward conclusions about his life.

One of Roger Patten's favorite passages was a discussion of the nature of hunger. Prather analyzes the sensation in the stomach as a sound that can be interpreted as tension. If one does not want to feed, the sensation can be alleviated, he writes, simply by performing a basic physical exercise. The similar, powerful urge for sex caused Prather to form attachments with several women. When he did not have intercouse with the women, he found the urge diminished. In hindsight, he thought he had misinterpreted his feelings, that the urge was a push toward companionship rather than mating. As Prather recorded these memories, he was alone in the mountains, and all of the sensations had left him. Consequently, he thought it logical that what he was feeling when he thought he wanted sex could just as well have been a desire for solitude. But these root causes, he continued, are not definitions but words. A sensation has individuality. An urge is not positive because it stems from emptiness. A desire, he concluded, is therefore mandated by a decision. The end of the syllogisms Prather built are sometimes pessimistic and can be of a profoundly fatal tone. Prather says that he is limited, life is just life, and what will be will be.

Notes on Love and Courage, written later, sounds a more hopeful note. Roger Patten seemed to prefer the second book, though he carried each of the two Prather volumes around in his back pocket through different periods.

The Velveteen Rabbit, however, was Roger's favorite story. Ostensibly for children, the book, written by Margery Williams and illustrated by William Nicholson, is short and takes about an hour to read. It is the tale of a cloth rabbit who is given as a present to a small boy. The boy loves the rabbit, and the toy endures various hardships for the boy, his friend. Sometimes when they play together the boy is good to him and they have fun; other times the youngster forgets all about the rabbit, and he lies outside all night where it is wet and cold.

"What is REAL?" asked the Rabbit one day. "Does it mean having things that buzz inside you and a stick-out handle?"

"Real isn't how you are made," said the Skin Horse. "It's a thing that happens to you. When a child loves you for a long, long time, not just to play with, but REALLY loves you, then you become Real. It doesn't happen all at once. You become. It takes a long time."

The story is a soliloquy about inner beauty transforming physical appearance, and it's in harmony with Prather's lessons stressing the triumph of an orderly inner nature over what may appear to be a rough exterior. Roger Patten asked his mother to read *The Velveteen Rabbit* and tell him what she thought it was about. She did. She doesn't remember now exactly how she responded, but she knows that Roger disagreed with her. When she asked him what he thought the story meant he just shook his head and said she wouldn't understand.

• • •

In the spring of 1978, the people around Roger Patten began to notice that he was changing. His odd jobs were petering out; one of the men he had worked for had sold his building, and Roger's family wasn't sure what happened to the others. His sister Suzen had broken up with her husband and moved into a furnished three-and-a-half-room apartment on Maplewood with her two toddlers. She tried to help Roger fill out job applications and asked people she knew to help him get work. But Roger didn't want a steady job, he said; he wanted work that was flexible; he wanted to be his own boss. He began getting day work at a place called Labor World. He became proficient at loading and unloading trucks in warehouses. For a period of several months he worked at a packing house on the south side. Somewhere along the line, his sister claims, he fell in with a bad crowd. He frequented a pool hall on the west side. Suzen noticed before other people did that he was now drinking. She doesn't drink herself, and she had been attuned to her father's habits when he was a practicing alcoholic.

Suddenly, Roger stopped eating. He lost weight rapidly. He took to drinking gallons of diet cola. No one saw him eat anything besides an occasional bowl of dry cereal. His gift-giving became even more compulsive. He seldom walked through the door without a present for one of Suzen's kids, an artificial tree for his parents' apartment, a throw pillow for the couch. His sleep patterns became erratic. His mother would find him scrubbing the kitchen floor at two o'clock in the morning. He told her that he didn't like to go to sleep because he had a recurring nightmare. Roger spent more time reading his books and sitting at the beach by himself. If he had any friends at all, he didn't speak of them. Inside of a few months, he dropped sixty pounds. His mother, who was worried that he wasn't getting the vitamins he needed, urged him to have some food—some soup, anything. Roger refused. His clothes began to hang on him, but he seemed to be as discouraged about his appearance as ever. Even with the approach of summer and warmer weather, he remained bundled up in shirts and jackets. He became weak, and by the fall of 1978 he could no longer work.

When his parents moved from the building on Ainslie into an apartment on West Fullerton, near Governor Jim Thompson's Chicago home, Roger moved into a north-side YMCA. But that arrangement lasted only about a week. He appeared at his parents' place with his suitcase full of belongings and divided his time between his sister's apartment on Maplewood and his parents' new home in Lincoln Park. His eldest brother Craig moved into the same building where Suzen was living, and his brother David, after serving two years and nine months, was released on parole. David also took a furnished apartment in the Maplewood building.

By the time Christmas rolled around, Roger had lost almost a hundred pounds and was totally paranoid. He had painted one of the cast-iron model guns black with a magic marker, and he carried the gun with him at all times. He got the idea that somebody was following him, that people were out to get him. He began to look sick and sleepy. Then George Patten had another heart attack and was hospitalized at Augustana for a couple of weeks. Roger's drinking became more of a problem. He went from periods of hyperactivity to times when he could barely move, when he would just sit in the living room and stare at the television. His father had been back at home for about a week when Roger made what his father calls a "half-assed attempt" to commit suicide, by swallowing a bottle of Dilantin, prescription medicine that George Patten was taking for his heart condition. The Dilantin made Roger very sick, but it didn't kill him. Roger's stomach was pumped at Swedish Covenant Hospital, and the doctor there recommended that Roger see a doctor he knew of at the Institute of Psychiatry of Northwestern Hospital. Roger Patten was admitted to the psychiatric ward. He began taking Thorazine and started therapy. He made some friends at the hospital, one of them a girl.

• • •

Roger Patten's previous encounters with girls had been disastrous. After he lost weight, the situation had worsened. Because he had dropped so much weight so fast, his skin sagged. He wore a binder to hide the fact that he had developed breasts, and Suzen learned after his death that he sometimes wore a girdle too. He was terrified to undress in front of anyone. He had tried it only once, and the girl had laughed at him. Roger hoped to impress the girl at the hospital with his sensitivity, and he labored long afternoons trying to write letters to her. His father helped him, showing him how to use the dictionary and giving him the spellings of various words. For practice, Roger started copying passages from some of his books.

Suzen has a tablet that belonged to Roger. It reads:

"Notes on Love and Courage by Hugh Prather . . . copyed [sic] by Roger T. Patten. I can't be found in myself; I discover myself in others.

That much is clear. And I suspect that I also love and care for myself in others . . . . All these people passing by. Every year another ocean of faces I will never see again. By using my eyes I can connect with a few, but only a few. And even that is often misunderstood. . . . There is another way to go through life besides being pulled through it kicking and screaming. . . .

Roger was admitted to the hospital several times during the winter. Once, while he was staying there, he loaned his razor to a friend who was in a room nearby. The friend slit his throat with Roger's razor. Roger was ridden with guilt.

●   ●   ●

During the times he was living at home or out of the hospital on weekend passes, he became closer to his brother David. He looked up to David, he told his sister, because David was street smart; he had learned to be tough while he was doing time in Pontiac. Roger's moods vacillated wildly. His mother noticed once that he was unable to concentrate enough to keep track of the plot of a film he was watching on television. Some nights he could be the model son, waiting for his mother to get off work, walking her home through a blizzard, and rubbing her shoulders until she was relaxed enough to go to sleep. Then he would disappear for hours at a time and return home dead drunk. His nightmares terrified him. He told his mother that when he drank he could sleep without dreaming. He was filled with anger, he said.

He went back into the hospital. While he was there, he took to shredding empty tin cans, so his doctor gave him clay, a less dangerous substitute. When he asked to go home, the staff at Northwestern advised him not to, and he had to sign a form that said in part: "I acknowledge that I have been informed of the risks involved to my life and health; I hereby agree to assume those risks and the consequences of my conduct. Furthermore, I release the attending physician, the hospital, and its staff from all responsibility for any ill effects which may result from this action."

For a couple of weeks Roger seemed to get better. "One day when we're alone and I feel better, I'll explain something to you," Roger told his mother. Joan Patten urged him to tell her right away. "Even if you can only say it one word at a time," she insisted. When Roger refused, she added, "You know I'll always be here." Roger decided to take an apartment in the building with Suzen, Craig, and David. Suzen took him to the local Social Security office and helped him with his application for welfare. He moved into the new place in the beginning of March.

"You'll see, I'm going to make it this time," he told his family. At first, he seemed interested in having his own apartment. His folks gave him some record albums, a television, a clock radio, some pots and pans. Suzen put up draperies for him. Then one night, his brother David borrowed one of Roger's real-looking guns and tried to rob the Diplomat Motel on North Lincoln Avenue.

"CID Unit 8618 responded to a radio call of a Robbery in Progress at the above motel," the police report says. "Upon arrival the victim clerk was interviewed. Mr. Trograncic explained that a M/W subject entered the motel office asking for a room. Moments later the offender standing at the far end of the counter displayed a handgun demanding money from the register. The victim complied and handed over to the offender an undetermined amt. of currency.

"The victim explained that, as the subject was pointing the gun at him, he managed to grab the gun and overpower the offender, grabbing the gun with one hand and grabbing the subject's coat with the other hand. In the scuffle, the barrel of the gun snapped in two, alerting the victim to the fact that the gun was not real. Victim, holding subject with one hand, pushed him down into a nearby chair while dialing police with his free hand. According to the victim, however, the offender managed to flee the motel office leaving behind his jacket, shirt, and misc. ID in the jacket. Subject slipped out of the jacket, thereby running bare-chested from the motel office. Also left behind was a quantity of U.S. currency, which was immediately returned to the motel clerk, upon the arrival of the undersigned and responding Patrol Units."

The report goes on to say that the police examined the identification belonging to David Patten and that a radio broadcast went out. Within minutes, two other police officers returned to the motel with David, who was informed of his rights and placed under arrest. Three days went by before George Patten learned that David was back in Cook County Jail. Policeman Carl was the only memeber of the family who got to see or talk to David at first. Five days after his arest, Suzen got a letter from David:

"By now you've probably already heard the news of my being back in the County Jail. I'm not even going to try and explain because right now it feels like I'm asleep, and everything that happened, is a bad dream. When the police caught me, they took me to Belmont and Western Police Station. The cops busted my head open in three places, broke my hand, busted my eye, and gave me scars on my back from a rubber hose. I showed Carl what they did to me, and he said he'd look into it for me. I should of wrote yesterday, but I really didn't know what to write without it sounding stupid. After I reached the County Jail, I was thinking real hard about killing myself, but I know I don't have the nerve to kill myself. Sure I know I fucked up a good thing. I had it made, and believe me I'm not here because I want to be. It's almost killing me inside knowing I'll have to go back to the Joint for about five years, but what kills me more is knowing that you, mom and dad had such high hopes for me, and I ended up crushing them. I guess dad's right, once a fuck-up, always a fuck-up. I was really growing to love Scottie and Amy, their [sic] beautiful children, and I was really happy for the first time in about ten years. Hug the kids for me for about ten minutes, don't let them know that their uncle David's in jail, tell them I'm on vacation in Florida or something. After all these years it really felt good getting along with dad, I always hoped we could get back together. But even though it was for a short time, it was worth a Billion Dollars. Well Sue, I'm gonna stop here before I start crying like a big jerk. Take care of yourself, and please always remember, I love you and mom and dad with all my heart."

Because David had used Roger's gun in the robbery, Roger considered himself responsible for what had happened. He refused to discuss his brother with anyone in the family. He started to drink again. He wandered around in a stupor. He was sick to his stomach and lost control of his bladder. He would get on the bus and get lost. His rage was now directed at the police. He hated Carl, his policeman brother, for disowning the family. He hated the police who had arrested David for beating him. He checked into the hospital for a few days, carrying a box with a fifth of whiskey, a butcher knife, and another fake pistol. When he left Northwestern he took the paraphernalia with him. He told his brother Craig that he wouldn't be around for long. He told his father that he was going to buy him a nice pipe for Father's Day so he could use it to get off cigarettes.

Then he went to the beach with his phony gun and attracted the police.

127

"We should have known what was going to happen when he told Craig he was going to die, that he would go through with it. If he told somebody something, he had to do it," Suzen says. "If Roger said he was going to do your laundry or something, he'd go through with it. He would feel committed."

A couple of hours after Roger was killed, authorities telephoned Suzen and asked her to come and identify the body. Suzen called her mother at about eleven o'clock, and they took a cab to the morgue. Carl was already there. He came to the waiting room in tears. He hadn't seen his brother since before he had lost weight. "He looks like me when I was sixteen or seventeen," he told them. That night Suzen went up to Roger's apartment to start moving his things out.

"I sat there and I looked around," she says. "Maybe Roger didn't think he had anything to live for. But he did."

Weeks after the funeral, George Patten still couldn't understand what had happened. Why, he wondered, did his youngest son, who had never seen the inside of a police station, get killed? Why did a policeman have to shoot Roger in the back of the head? Why was David beaten in the first place? He asked anyone who would listen. He called the Office of Professional Standards (OPS). He called the local chapter of the ACLU. He told the story of what had happened to two of his sons, and all the people who heard it shook their heads and said how sorry they were. One fellow, a casual acquaintance, commented on the frustration that somebody who's been through what George Patten had been through must feel. How awful it must be, he said, to feel so "ineffective."

● ● ●

The OPS has finished its investigation of the incident involving David Patten. George Patten will receive official notification saying that, if he wants to get a lawyer and press charges, the agency's files can be opened to him by subpoena. Robert Wooldridge says that the incidence of police shootings has dropped dramatically in the years since 1970. "The police have in excess of 11 million contacts a year," he says. "They arrest 60,000 people who are charged with felonies, and they confiscate 20,000 guns. Last year there were 79 shootings. Measure 79 shootings against 20,000 guns."

Robert Wooldridge thinks the story of the Patten boy is very, very sad. He feels sorry for George Patten, and he understands how upset he is. He shakes his head and calls the whole mess a terrible tragedy. The chief administrator in the OPS, James Casey, feels the same way. There is really nothing much to say.

● ● ●

It is not easy to keep a distance from poverty and violence and sudden death in Chicago. A man in a wheelchair, attending his own divorce hearing in the county building, pulls a gun from his lap and shoots his lawyer and the judge. The attorney, a young man with children, is awake and alive as he is taken from the building on a stretcher. Within the hour he is dead. The police lift the man who killed him, still in his wheelchair, into a waiting paddy wagon. This happened on television.

A suburban man barricades himself in his home with his two small children. The police wait for hours, attempting to negotiate, hoping he will sober up. But he does not—he murders his babies before he kills himself. The shots ring out on the six o'clock news.

People carry guns and get wildly drunk and become frightened and go nuts. A policeman may take someone's life. And sometimes civilians murder policemen.

But whether we are near or far away, we have this one thing in common: Everybody is just so damn ineffective.

5

Counsel For The Defense

Allan Ackerman, one of a small number of successful criminal lawyers in Chicago, traffics in love and death on a daily basis. He has made a career defending violence-prone bikers, Cuban dope peddlers, and white-collar extortionists. His clients have almost invariably reached a kind of impasse. Circumstances, usually of their own making, will irreparably change their lives. Though his business has hardened him, Allan Ackerman has a sense that everything he does is important to someone. Allan Ackerman, with his vivid descriptions and sense of humor, was the person who introduced me to the judicial system. Understanding the courts has, in a sense, made me a patriot. Most significant modern dramas, I found out, are not onstage in a theater; they are played out in a courtroom somewhere.

As you step through the door and into the office, the only visible piece of Allan Ackerman is his talking head. At first glance you might miss the animate mouth amid the debris of other, inanimate faces that crowd the narrow room. There are metal-covered heads filled with plaster, dressed in sunglasses and jaunty feathered hats; there's a canvas head of Shakespeare and the painted head of a clown; there are heads on clothed and unclothed bodies and heads of plastic paperweight people and photographs of heads on the walls. Holed up in the rear of the space, dwarfed by the proliferation of heads, the live head appears to be operating independently of any body, perched atop the imposing wooden desk along with books, newspapers, old birthday cards, layers of dust, unopened bottles of wine, cardboard boxes, legal briefs bound in plastic, pamphlets, magazines, and empty containers that once secured perishable substances. Framed documents indicating honors, group affiliations, and official credentials and statues, bumper stickers, and posters with pithy sayings circa 1966 surround it.

The head is talking into a telephone receiver. Its features are large and swollen-looking and its jaw pins the instrument to a shoulder. A small shock of black hair rests on a forehead that would be too much for any other face. The complexion has been tanned to a swarthy glow. The mouth works quickly, quietly, efficiently, making low, purring sounds almost inaudible in the din of country music that floats from one of two digital clock radios in the bookcase, to Shakespeare's left. A few more purrs, then an oversized hand attached to a long arm emerges from beneath the desktop, grabs the receiver from the neckline cradle, and slams it down behind the head. As part of the same motion, a wiry body rises from a huge chair. Allan Abel Ackerman, attorney at law, makes his way nimbly across the room, careful not to upset any of the litter. He grabs his yellow coffee mug and steps out for a refill.

Certain spots in Ackerman's office, a personal museum that has been almost twenty years in the making, are reserved for his own use. Other spots are offered to visitors and clients. Of the five chairs—all overworked leather or heavy-duty woven material—three are interchangeable. The couch, sagging beneath cartons of trial transcripts, has fallen into disuse. Ackerman chooses for himself places with a view. When he is conversing with a live person, he prefers to sit with his back to the door, facing the trashy desk and the diplomas on the far wall. He talks across a wooden table piled with a supplementary mess. Over his head, the client can see two views of a naked woman and a reproduction of an old English cartoon featuring a bunch of barristers. When he is alone in the office, on the phone or writing or studying, he sits at the rear and faces the door, lord of all he surveys.

Ackerman is a gnome-king making odds; he deals in points and percentages, factors and procedures, subtle psychology and complicated legal precedents. He is a lawyer in the crime business, one of the best in the city, his colleagues say, and one of the most successful (his income is into six figures). There are about 14,000 lawyers in Chicago, and according to American Bar Foundation data, only 6 percent spend the greatest amount of their time practicing criminal law; of those the vast majority are employed by the government. Ackerman himself estimates that he is one of about thirty private lawyers in Chicago working full-time to keep people out of jail.

"Anybody who goes to law school will tell you that 75 percent of the students consider going into criminal law," Ackerman says. "It's supposed to be exciting, glamorous. When you get into it you find out that 60 percent of it is research, 20 percent is investigating and interviewing clients, and the other aspect of it is the written work. You don't have much of a social life. You deal with would-be mobsters and Cuban dope peddlers. Most criminal lawyers are divorced. [Ackerman has been divorced three times.] Most work twelve to fourteen hours a day, and for the time they put in they are grossly underpaid. I argued in front of juries most of the time in 1977 and probably tried six cases and won three and lost three. To win three, you're beating the odds."

● ● ●

Drug cases take up about half of Ackerman's extended workday. Search and seizure, entrapment, and other pesky Fourth Amendment issues have become his field of expertise, if only out of necessity. Dope trials are what set the odds so high against him. As he explains, it is not an easy task to keep someone on the street after he's been indicted on a heroin charge.

"You're starting with such an inherent prejudice. It's not like counterfeiting or stolen securities. You try a marijuana case, big deal. Cocaine, everybody reads about it everywhere. But you start talking anywhere from three to twenty pounds of heroin. . . . You show me a lawyer who'll put heroin before a jury, and you're showing me an asshole. Any number of times the lawyer who doesn't know, doesn't understand, takes the money and pleads them guilty. In a drug case, generally you've got one very experienced prosecutor, one inexperienced prosecutor, and a well-trained agent. If they come in and put a pound of heroin on the table, what are the odds the client is going to get a fair trial?

"There's even more to it. Heroin often involves Spanish-speaking people. I don't speak it, so I'm always dealing with an interpreter. There are excellent ones, but you always lose something. Particularly when they're trying to tell you how law agents and informers trapped them into a situation."

Even if Ackerman gets the story straight, the courtroom proceedings can become very weird in narcotics-related cases. The same people keep showing up in different circumstances. Ackerman's firm—Ackerman, Durkin, and Egan—is one of the downtown law firms retained by the Chicago Federation of Police. Often they represent police officers accused by the city of verbal or physical abuse. Then, sometime later, they find their former clients testifying against them in another trial. "We've had to withdraw many times from situations where for one reason or another there's a conflict of interest. With drug cases you frequently get a conflict because your client last year turns out to be an informer this year."

Three-quarters of the pending matters piled up in Ackerman's outer office are cases on appeal, and about 70 percent of those span the last four and a half years. In addition to the drug cases, there is a whole mishmash of illegal activities. Stolen securities. Attempted murder. ("This has to do with a person's being competent to stand trial," Ackerman says, tossing a brief on the table.) Perjury. Attempt to kill a policeman. . . .

• • •

One of the phones by the back wall begins buzzing. Ackerman pushes a button and issues a loud hello into the mouthpiece. "Your son was taken into custody," he says. He listens for a moment. "They didn't say anything about a car. . . ." He slumps farther down in his chair and rubs his hands on his brow. "I'm asking for the bond to be set at $700." He says yes a couple of times and hangs up.

Criminal lawyers, by all accounts, cannot deal with simple guilt or innocence. The situations are too bizarre, the subtleties too complex. "Fully half the cases fall into a loose category," Ackerman says. " 'Loose' is the word I use for the defendant being conned into it by an informer who doesn't give a damn as long as there's an arrest." The briefs that Ackerman presents for appeals in such cases are extraordinary. Legal briefs are traditionally the driest, most tedious literature to see print, noteworthy only because it's difficult to figure out how anybody but the most mindless could read them at all. They are always painful for a defense attorney, and Ackerman is no exception. But some of his briefs have an unusual quality, a sense of amazement, or perhaps even amusement, at the complicated maneuvers of law enforcement.

Consider the plight of poor Juan Trevino Luna, busted by federal agents for narcotics. Allan wrote a brief full of pretrial motions for dismissal of the indictment.

D.E.A. [U.S. Drug Enforcement Administration], an informer, and the government provide the sanctity for the background of this case. In tender terms we commence. Sometime in 1976, D.E.A. agents (probably Agent Tucci among others) arrested a handsome but vicious person named Francisco. [A footnote says, "Tall and handsome he is . . . mean and vicious he is."] In an indescribable fashion (because we don't know), D.E.A. and Francisco entered into a union. Francisco was to produce cases and the government would 'front him off' before the trial judge from whom Francisco's case was then pending. Francisco was represented by counsel, *albeit* we eschew any opportunity to suggest that Francisco's attorney was within the parameters of the D.E.A.–Francisco shenanigans. Agent Tucci and the D.E.A. are interested in making cases, and Francisco accommodated. His thespian talents are part and parcel of this motion. In addition, he is (was) a paid informer.

2. *Scene I, Act 1:* In the late spring or early summer of 1976 Francisco was utilizing his charm and talent in attempting to compromise a woman, Maria Cruz. It seems that after an evening of drinking and dancing Francisco and Ms. Cruz ended up in a motel in Cicero, Illinois. After a "Peyton Place" *lovemaking session* Francisco called Tucci. Tucci ceremoniously entered the motel room and was apparently introduced as either friend or relative of Francisco. The "ruse" continued from there. The saga indicated (indeed demonstrated) that Ms. Cruz, at the less than gentle urging of Francisco, was successful in securing the quantity of heroin for Agent Tucci on or about September 20, 1976, in Chicago, Illinois. Ms. Cruz was rewarded. She was indicted (*U.S. v. Cruz, et al.,* 76 CR 1063). That, if the Court pleases, is the beginning of a series of events which will be the subject (hopefully) of a lengthy hearing before this Court which would have its predicate on "outrageous government misconduct."

3. Post-indictment, Ms. Cruz and Francisco met, from time to time, in saloons in Cicero, Illinois. On one of these occasions Francisco was seen with *Luna*. Apparently Ms. Cruz attempted to speak to Luna. From what can be presently ascertained, she was going to warn *Luna* that Francisco was probably an informer. This event occurred somewhere around Thanksgiving, 1976. Our modern day melodrama continued with a subplot. This subplot included the necessity (apparently) that *Luna* not learn of Francisco's nexus with *Tucci*. Francisco solved this dilemma by spiriting Ms. Cruz off to a local motel where physical contact occurred. She was threatened with all manner of harm (she has three [3] children) were she to reveal to Luna anything about Francisco. Ms. Cruz will testify that the innkeeper called the local constables because of the noise from the motel room and that the police arrived. The police left after consulting with Francisco. In any event, strange as it may seem, Ms. Cruz had only a single phone number to contact

Francisco. That phone number turned out to be the place where Luna worked. We retreat for a moment. Luna has been employed by International Harvester for about ten (10) years. Francisco was employed there for some months and that is where Luna and Francisco met. Luna himself is not an uncomely male. Apparently Ms. Cruz has a penchant for "falling for" handsome Hispanic males. In any event, Ms. Cruz failed to warn or communicate to Luna the background of Francisco and thus Francisco imposed upon Luna to attempt to secure controlled substances.

• • •

This brief, presented to Judge Prentice Marshall, continues to describe in melodramatic terms how Luna ended up selling dope to Maria Cruz's boyfriend Francisco and got himself indicted for it. Ackerman suggests a government conspiracy, the conspirators being Francisco, Tucci, and "others unknown to Luna" and the purpose of the charade being to get a couple of indictments for the D.E.A. and a suspended sentence for that handsome devil Francisco. "Taken together (or even apart), we have the D.E.A. and a fee-splitting, indicted informer, already on probation (for homicide) in a conspiratorial union. Francisco 'entrapped' Ms. Cruz with his charm and body. . . . How much of all this D.E.A. knew or didn't know will, of course, be the subject of a hearing."

The cases against the hapless Maria Cruz (who insisted through the whole thing that she loved Francisco) and Juan Luna were both thrown out of court.

The law, you see, can be made to work on behalf of the good guys—or, at least, the marginal guys—the same way it can work for the bad guys who have a good lawyer. Ackerman explains, "I got out of law school, and I thought I knew a lot of law. I did know a lot of law. But that's not all there is to it. That was explained to me by an older, experienced lawyer."

Ackerman gives an example of how the law works:

"This is a table, is it not?"

"This is a table."

"How do you know that this is a table?"

"That's a table because it fits the definition of *table* that I was taught."

"You were taught that a table has four legs, were you not?"

"I was taught that a table has four legs."

"That desk over there has four legs; therefore, that desk must be a table too."

"The desk is not a table."

"Why is that desk not a table?"

"The desk is not a table because it does not fit the definition of *table* that I was taught."

"A dog has four legs; is a dog a table?"

"No, a dog is not a table because it does not fit the definition of *table* that I was taught."

"What if the definition of *table* you were taught was wrong? Then could a dog be a table?"

"Possibly."

"If your teacher was wrong, could a desk be a table?"

"Sure."

"Then that desk could be a table and a dog could be a table, could they not?"

"Yes."

"I just got you to say that a desk or a dog could possibly be a table," Ackerman says. "See what I mean about the law?"

● ● ●

On Memorial Day afternoon Allan Ackerman is working. The 95-degree heat has taken Chicagoans, including downtown office building engineers gone for a long weekend, by surprise. The office at 100 N. LaSalle has no air. It's hotter inside than outside. Ackerman has just come back from the Federal Building, where he was checking out the original transcript from the Mitchell Edelson perjury trial, a conviction he will appeal on Thursday. Mitch Edelson is a disbarred lawyer facing a year in the federal penitentiary for perjury. He was convicted in April 1977 and sentenced June 17. A year ago he asked Ackerman if he would consider writing his appeal.

It was not the first Ackerman had heard of the Edelson business. Though he had retained another attorney for the trial, Edelson had periodically sought Ackerman's advice after his indictment in October 1975. The indictment was the result of Edelson's testimony before a grand jury the year before. Edelson was questioned about phone conversations between himself and a client, Roger, who turned out to be a government informer. The informer had taped the conversations. Roger had gone to trial himself in 1974, along with another man, Geoffrey Disston. Disston was convicted in that trial (as was Roger) and served a year and a half in prison.

Though Allan Ackerman was in no way connected to the original cases of Roger, Disston, or Mitch Edelson, by the end of 1975 he had some information about all three. He knew that the beef revolved around negotiations and stolen securities. Wiretapping was involved. He knew Roger was a government informer, possibly at the time he was tried along with Disston. In 1976 Disston wrote Ackerman a letter asking him to appeal his conviction. Ackerman went over and checked the records on Disston's case. It seemed to him that there was some doubt as to whether Disston had received a fair trial. Disston said he had no funds, so Ackerman asked that the court appoint him as counsel and grant Disston a new trial. A court-appointed counsel gets paid by the federal government, $30 an hour for in-court work and $20 for out-of-court work. The court refused, but Ackerman decided to go ahead with the appeal anyway. He also took Edelson's case and began making arrangements to argue the two cases with the same cast of characters on the same day.

Ackerman's upcoming appearance before the appeals judges has been literally years in the making. After conviction, the court sets a date when the appeals briefs will be due, generally about five weeks after trial transcripts become available. The average trial transcript is available thirty-five to forty days after the original trial; if the transcript is inordinately long, it may take fifteen or twenty days more. In Edelson's case the transcripts were not completed until November 1977. In the Disston case, Ackerman had moved for a new trial in June 1976; his motion was denied by the trial judge in November, and Ackerman filed a brief in the court of appeals the next year. The Edelson brief, ninety pages of it, was filed in the early part of 1978, after Ackerman asked for extra time to assemble his case. Then the prosecutors had thirty to forty days to file their briefs in response. Finally, the Thursday, June 1, date was set for the arguments in court. "You have an opportunity to file again within fifteen days if the government has filed something that's all wrong or improper in your opinion," Ackerman explains. "But if you're satisfied with what you wrote originally, you can just go ahead."

Though the meat of an appeal is in the writing of the briefs, a criminal lawyer generally enters an extended period of studying and reading just before the court date in hopes of anticipating what the panel of judges might say. Allan Ackerman is studying and reading on Memorial Day. He doesn't bitch about working on the holiday. He is at home in the place he holds most dear, even though his eighteen-hour-a-day work habit is probably to blame for his bevy of ex-wives and myriad other minor problems.

• • •

Ackerman says he is thirty-nine years old—though rumor has it he's a couple of years older—and doesn't go out much. Practicing law has taken up most of his past twenty years. Before that he went to four Chicago high schools, was dispatched from three, went to Wright Junior College, the University of Chicago, and John Marshall Law School. He was admitted to the bar in 1961 at age twenty-two. The same year, a lawyer who did a lot of personal injury cases took him on. He told Allan that he was too crazy and too weird to go out in public. "I was making $42.50 a week when I started with Johnny Phillips," Ackerman says. "He was one fine lawyer. After six months he bought me three suits and took me to court by the hand. He showed me how to be there." Ackerman left Phillips in 1962 and practiced by himself until 1970, when Tom Durkin left the State's Attorney's office to become Ackerman's partner. John Egan left the State's Attorney's office the following year and became the third partner. About 85 percent of the work they do is criminal, and the rest is civil. Egan and Durkin are the angel-faced sons of sturdy Irish stock. They are textbook examples of what a fine Chicago upbringing can turn out.

Ackerman is something else. His peers speak of him as a more-than-competent eccentric. He's small—somewhere in mid-air between five and six feet, but closer to five—and sexy. In the office he dresses to please himself. His outfits are jeans and T-shirts and boots. He has hair all over his chest. Sometimes he wears a shirt, and sometimes he doesn't. Other times he sort of wears a shirt. Even when it hasn't been fashionable, he's worn his hair long, and some of it curls over the edge of his collar. When he goes to court he shows some respect by donning a shirt, tie, and a jacket that matches the pants. A gold chain with a medallion hangs from his neck, and a ring he wears on his left hand is stamped with a set of scales. His appearance offends some of the people he works with, he admits, but it appeals to others.

Ackerman's mode of dress holds little truck in court, where his reputation outweighs his looks, and has never caused raised eyebrows among clients, who are hardly socially acceptable themselves. In fact, Ackerman's manner in the office puts the most deviant of outcasts at ease. When he talks to them, he talks their language. "Twelve years ago, ten years ago, I was upstairs in this building. A guy as big as the door comes in without an appointment. My secretary Judy comes in and says, 'There's this big monster out there to see you.' Big Jim was his name. He comes in and he says, 'You Ackerman? I want to talk to you.' So he sits down with his chain belt and he says, 'We've got this little case here. Fat Cowboy and the other guys got cracked, and the coppers were wrong. That's enough. Look it up in the court records.' So I got out to look it up in Oak Lawn and Midlothian, and as far as I could figure out the police cracked them. I convinced the judge that the search was illegal."

Ackerman has pleaded a host of cases for the Outlaws and the D. C. Eagles motorcycle gangs. "Seven years ago I'm driving home on Lake Shore Drive and I see blue lights. There must have been sixty squad cars out there. When I get home I get a phone call. 'Johnny D. is in the hospital. There was a little shoot-out at Foster Avenue Beach.' A couple of warring factions shot it out. All of his complainants were bikers. They wouldn't go against each other."

● ● ●

At seven o'clock there's a knock at the door. A woman, approximately four foot ten, comes into the office. She explains that her husband worked at a Clark gas station. On Sunday morning he didn't come home. The sheriff's police called her and told her that her husband was gone and $2,800 was missing, she tells Allan. "But I know he didn't steal the money," she says. "He was kidnapped."

"Kidnapped?" says Ackerman. "How do you know he was kidnapped?"

"There was blood on the pillow in the car," she replies. "And, anyway, he called me collect from Lakewood, California."

"What's in Lakewood, California?"

"That's where his brother lives." She tells Ackerman that she is going to have the pillow analyzed and her husband is going to hitchhike home. She proceeds to give Ackerman a modest retainer. He is thinking of some questions that he won't ask. He is wondering what happened to the kidnappers, why they took her husband all the way to his brother's place in California, how come his brother won't give him any money to get home, and where she will get the money to retain a lawyer if her husband has to hitchhike back.

Allan Ackerman thinks maybe he doesn't need this kind of grief. He thinks about how he just got out of the hospital after a gall bladder removal and he has to argue two appeals in federal court in a couple of days. He shrugs, "The allegation is a breeze. Only $2,800." It's hotter than hell in this building.

•   •   •

Ackerman arrives at the 27th floor of the Everett Dirksen Building on Dearborn Street before noon on June 1. He wants to study the transcripts, the briefs, and the records from the court docket again. The whole shebang stands about three feet high when all the papers are stacked up. Around the corner from the bank of elevators, where locked double doors of frosted glass enclose the judge's chambers, is the office of the court clerk, and across from that are the doors to 2721, the courtroom. The attorney's room, the lawyer's green room, is to the right of the court. This is where Ackerman sits and reads and gets quietly tense waiting for 2 P.M. to come. He and his piles of papers are parked at one of two wooden parson's tables near the back of the room. Under other circumstances, it might be a comfortable place: the Bar Association has provided three good-sized palms, a couple of cacti, three brown leather loveseats, eight red tweed chairs, and a gallery of portraits of judges and past presidents of the organization.

But it's not comfortable in here today. It's stuffy, and the picture of Judge Walter J. Cummings, Jr., is bothering Ackerman, as it always does. If you sit at one of the tables, Cummings's eyes follow you no matter where you look. Cummings is a great guy, Ackerman admits. He even says that Cummings is one of his favorites. But his eyes follow you in court and his eyes follow you in the attorney's room, and it's just too much. Ackerman stands up and glares at the photograph. He decides he was right to call in the court clerk and complain. Anyone would have to agree, the photograph belongs on a different wall. He sits down again. He is wearing his "good suit"— a leisurely tan outfit with a lot of extra buttons—and a blue shirt and red tie. He's getting tired of reading. A young guy comes in from the clerk's office and says he'll send somebody in to pick up Ackerman's stuff in about half an hour. He returns about twenty minutes later.

About 1:30, Mitch Edelson arrives. He is wondering who the judges are going to be. Ackerman doesn't know. Usually he does, but there has been some shuffling around today and nobody's quite sure. Ackerman thinks William Bauer will be one of the three on the panel. Edelson talks to his lawyer in low tones. He says he's lost seven or eight pounds in the last week. His face is beginning to redden. Other lawyers begin milling around in the hall, talking and chuckling. "Four minutes to post," Ackerman says, joining the group outside. He shakes hands with several of the government prosecutors. Their moods are deadly serious as they take their seats on opposite sides of the courtroom. They are going to argue about whether or not Mitch Edelson, another lawyer, should go to jail. It won't be amusing.

At 2:02, a middle-aged black man smartly dressed in a green suit signals for the court to rise. Judge Bauer takes his seat on the far right of the bench. He is followed by Judge Wilbur Pell, who is followed by Judge Philip Tone. A handful of lawyers and Edelson's son make up the audience. Everyone sits down at the same time.

Two minutes is enough time for total sensory assault in the federal court of appeals. The room is a luxurious imitation of Holy Name Cathedral. The dark wooden walls appear to stop about twenty feet up and open onto heaven: the lighting is so translucent it has to have been made by Mother Nature. This gives the judges, who sit at an elevated podium, a supernatural look, the closest earthly thing to the Holy Trinity since St. Patrick discovered shamrocks. The wooden benches for the spectators are spare enough, but the beige carpeting covering the huge expanse of room is not. Ackerman is sitting on the left side of the room at a table that is bigger than he is, in one of the dozen or so chairs that might be comfortable if they didn't carry so much authority. The three men at the prosecutor's table are in his direct line of sight. Behind each of the tables are little clusters of men in suits. The effect of these tax dollars at work is extraordinary. There is total silence: an awe hangs over the court. All eyes are riveted on the panel of judges, who already seem wise and wonderful and much better-looking than the average person.

They will hear about Geoffrey Disston first. The judges call Ackerman to the podium, and he faces them, standing between the two wooden tables. He plans to start slow today. With two cases to present—at least a half hour of talking for Ackerman and another half hour for the government—it will be a long session, and Ackerman knows, if the judges become disenchanted immediately, it will be a tough row to hoe. Judge Tone, a white-haired, almost classic-looking fellow, speaks first. He wants to know why Ackerman is appealing this case anyway. Did the court appoint him? Did Disston retain him? Is Disston in jail, out of jail, or what? Ackerman explains that Disston is through doing his time and doesn't have any money, but that he wanted to go through with it anyway. Bauer declares the technical status he's describing: "You've been retained, but your fee is kind of low," he says, terminating the discussion. Ackerman proceeds, recapitulating the material in his brief. In their written response to this brief, the prosecution has already conceded some of Ackerman's points, so it's a pretty simple explanation. He tells why he asked for another hearing in the Disston case, why the prosecution may have been wrong in keeping secret their relationship with the other defendant (Roger) originally tried with Disston, and, finally, why the charges against Disston should be dismissed.

After Ackerman's fifteen minutes are up, a government lawyer in a beige suit goes before the judges. He really doesn't give Ackerman much of an argument. His pitch is that, instead of dismissing the case, the appeals judges should order an evidentiary hearing before the judge of the original trial. "Why did the government take so long to see the light?" Tone wants to know. Bauer scribbles something down and passes it along to the other two judges. Pell questions the wisdom of another hearing before the same judge who tried the case. "Perhaps he wouldn't be able to see the forest for the trees," he suggests. They ask Ackerman a few more questions; he reiterates his burning desire for a dismissal and returns to his table.

Barely twenty minutes have gone by before Ackerman introduces the second argument, on behalf of Mitch Edelson. He opens with an apology for the length of his brief. Ackerman, Tone, and Pell engage in a little friendly banter about long briefs, then Ackerman gets to a discussion of some fine points of law that may or may not have been violated in the original perjury trial. Again, he's questioning the validity of certain evidence because of the way it was obtained and the bizarre circumstances leading to the trial. Edelson has turned a bright red; he is sitting in the front row of benches on the prosecution side of the aisle with his arms outstretched, a stack of legal papers beside him. Ackerman is standing up straight with his legs apart and moving his hands unobtrusively from the podium to his sides, occasionally crossing them behind his back. He speaks confidently and succinctly for twenty-five minutes.

Charles Wehner, representing the U.S. Attorney's office, is a large man somewhat reminiscent of Governor Thompson. He stretches out his arms and leans into the podium. His rebuttal doesn't take long. Ackerman, he assures the court, is trying to make something out of nothing. Pell and Tone begin questioning him closely about the points Ackerman has just raised. Bauer wants to know if there were any other indictments handed down at the time Edelson was indicted for perjury. Wehner says that there were. Pell says, in reference to an informer for the prosecution, "He was an independent contractor, but you didn't tell him what kind of paintbrushes to use. . . ." The prosecutor agrees. Ackerman returns to the podium.

"Are you arguing on this appeal that the district court erred in not letting you bring up the issue of materiality?" Judge Tone asks. Ackerman agrees with this summary. And it's quarter after three and it's all over. Everyone stands up again, the judges file out the door. Edelson and some of the other lawyers rush over to Ackerman, who doesn't say much, nods a few times, gathers some papers, and starts to leave. As he walks down the corridor he shakes his head to indicate he doesn't have anything to say to some people, gives others knowing glances, and merely greets the rest. He asks a young lawyer from his office what time it is and continues his march to the elevators. Once inside, he leans his arm up against the wall and looks at his feet. "Now," he says, "they think about it."

• • •

Mitch Edelson's appeal was a success, of sorts. The decision, whether it's won or lost, will not be known until next week or next year, but Ackerman is satisfied with the bit of theater he's scripted and starred in. He thinks he did the best he could.

"You always reflect on what you might have argued or how you might have answered a question best. Twenty percent of the outcome depends on the lawyer. I was taught to respond directly, crisply, and truthfully and never to quarrel with the panel of judges. All three are scholarly and reasonable people. For 99 percent of the people involved in federal convictions, this [the Seventh Circuit Court of Appeals] is the Supreme Court; the chances of getting into the Supreme Court of the United States are one in five hundred."

It's a serious business, yet Ackerman's success in it seems to depend a lot on a sense of humor. If you're dealing with a subterranean culture and talking jive part of the time, and playing a high-stakes game in the very technical realm of legalese the rest of the time, you will go bananas if you don't weed out what's funny and cherish it. That's why this off-the-wall amalgamation of stuff decorates Ackerman's office. That's why he keeps the newspaper clipping from the time he successfully defended the alleged California marijuana users by discrediting the government witness, a German shepherd named Ginger who sniffed out the dope. (Ginger didn't make it in court. When she took the stand she couldn't answer any questions. Besides, she had made a recent appearance on *Dragnet*, which may have prejudiced the jury.) That's why he relishes the story of the three men, "two Polacks and an Italian," who were charged with counterfeiting. Ackerman got them off, and they wanted to pay him in cash. That's why he appreciates Judy Lutes, the millionaire lottery winner, who still comes in and secretaries for him at 6:00 A.M. everyday. She's funny. And then there's his flaky, civic-minded mother in Florida. She's funny too. And the ex-wife who took the money instead of the property and periodically ends up stuck for a place to live. You have to laugh or cry. So you dress like an outlaw and talk like a stone intellectual; there's humor there somewhere.

● ● ●

Last week, Allan Ackerman was in front of Judge Hubert Will, dressed pretty much the way he's dressed all the time. It was a last-minute deal—a client of his on probation was picked up—and he could either change clothes and be late or go in as he was. Well, this client was convicted on a gun-running charge, and he hired Ackerman to appeal, and while he's out on probation his wife splits for West Virginia with the kids. So the guy tells his probation officer he's going to visit the family, and he follows the wife and snatches the three-year-old. The wife calls the FBI; she calls the probation officer; she calls everybody. When they find the guy he has to go back to court to explain why his probation shouldn't be revoked. After all, he lied about the purpose of his trip, and he kidnapped the kid.

By the time this whole mess gets to court, Judge Will is screaming. (The wife has called him too.) The probation officer is going nuts. "You're making me an accomplice to a kidnapping," the judge is saying. "You're out on my probation, and you're stealing a kid."

And the guy is saying. "It's my kid. I saw the kid. If you saw the kid, you would have grabbed too."

The judge is saying that this guy is never going anywhere again without his permission. He doesn't want to be aiding and abetting a federal crime. Judge Will doesn't like getting fifteen minutes of hell from the wife. The wife says he can come back and bring the kid if he promises not to steal any kids anymore. Judge Will wants to know if Ackerman has anything to say.

"Let him off probation," he offers meekly. Judge Will gives him an oh-you've-got-to-be-kidding laugh. The guy returns the kid and comes back to Chicago and reports to court.

●   ●   ●

At 9:00 P.M. on the day of the Edelson appeal hearing, Allan Ackerman is finally getting ready to go home. The Mexican whose trial is coming up didn't show up like he was supposed to. The black musician busted on a heroin charge dropped in for a visit even though he wasn't expected. ("I believe you," Ackerman tells him.) "If it wasn't for my clients I wouldn't eat," Ackerman says as he packs up to leave. "The other side of it is that it's just so insane that there's no way." He is going home to his condominium on the North Shore. Out of the five years he's owned the place, he's probably lived there a total of two. Sometimes he just doesn't want to hang around with the various and sundry people who insist on moving in. But he does like the place. It has marble floors.

"Any understanding as to what happened or what didn't happen in any given criminal case is probably coincidental," he says on the way out. "The whole atmosphere [of my life] is not conducive to the practice of criminal law."

6

The Life And Times Of The Cook County Morgue

Dr. Robert Stein, medical examiner and for almost a quarter of a century chief pathologist for Cook County, has seen everything. He is paid about $100,000 a year for his services, and he and his staff come under constant scrutiny by the press. Yet Stein and the people who work for him have one of the least desirable jobs in the city. They must retrieve valuable information from the sickness and sadness of death so that the rest of us may live longer and healthier lives. They are forced to view the destruction caused by the worst side of human behavior and yet are expected to discharge their duties with compassion and empathy for their fellow humans. They are guardians of the living, perceived as sentinels of death. A young investigator in Stein's office told me the worst thing he ever saw was the aftermath of a crash of a DC-10 that killed about 300 people. Yet it was not sifting through the wreckage for pieces of the bodies that disturbed him. It was sowing the tons of nails into the earth at the crash site; it was Dr. Stein's job to see to it that no treasure hunters would come along with metal detectors looking for valuables left behind.

One sunny afternoon, the third Thursday in January, 1983, Allen Dorfman, insurance man for the mob, was shot to death in the parking lot of a hotel-restaurant complex in north suburban Lincolnwood. The local police removed the body from the area in record time; in fact, a little pool of blood on the pavement was all that was left for the newsmen and ghouls when they descended on the site minutes later. Because he had died an "unnatural" death, the former Mr. Dorfman was soon delivered into the custody of Dr. Robert J. Stein, medical examiner for Cook County.

If you had to name a class of people who die from unnatural causes more often than anyone else, gangsters would be an obvious choice. So it's appropriate that gangster murders were the main reason Dr. Stein became interested in pathology in the first place. As a teenager growing up in the Bronx, Stein was so intrigued with the New York City mob wars of the 1920s that he cleaned the autopsy tables in the morgue there for free.

Fifty years later, Stein is still eyeing dead gangsters: down in the basement mortuary at the Morris Fishbein Institute of Forensic Medicine, the moldering kingdom he has ruled since 1976, he peels back the skin from the dead man's face and slices him open from neck to pelvis, working out the precise mechanisms of his death.

The morgue, a squat and faded three-story brick box that sits in the shadows behind Cook County Hospital, was built during Prohibition, when gangland slaughter was all the rage; Dorfman is just the latest in a long line of Cook County mobsters and their associates to be processed here. Most of them passed from this world without the benefit of a medical examiner—before Stein, the county operated on the coroner system, as many counties downstate still do. One of the first was Al Capone's brother Frank, who was rubbed out in Cicero in 1926, shortly after the morgue opened, one of nearly 300 shooting deaths that year.

There's more to history than death, I suppose, but when you've seen as much death as the county morgue has, you've seen a lot of history. The gangsters came here; so did their victims. The politicians came, and a few unlucky captains of industry, and, of course, the working people of the city—men, women, and children—a ceaseless parade of the dead.

The parade stops soon. By summer, Stein will have abandoned this place for a new institute of forensic medicine that he inspired and we paid for.*

• • •

The old building does not look particularly ominous from the outside, scarcely noticeable at all next to County's Gothic lines and awesome proportions, the modern brick towers and tunnels of the Rush-Presbyterian-Saint Luke's complex to the east, and the older, slightly more elegant buildings of the University of Illinois medical school to the south. The institute looks like what it was intended to be, an auxiliary place, an appendage. It looks like it should be a haven of patronage engineers, checking humming metal boxes and temperature gauges and reading the newspapers. But this is not a place anybody would come to to loaf around.

The odor would be surprising if you happened into the institute by accident. There have been many attempts to describe the stench; most of them end by calling it "indescribable" or "unmistakable" or by saying, "you'll know it when you smell it." It has been called sickly sweet, a gross underestimation. It is the smell of dried-up blood and fluids and putrefaction—a combination of diaper pail and compost

---

*This story was written shortly before the Cook County Medical Examiner's Office moved to its new home at the end of 1983.

heap and a little bit more. It's not so awful that you couldn't get used to it. People get used to it all the time. But it stays in your head for weeks: you'll catch a whiff of it on the subway and realize that one of your fellow riders has somehow started to decay. Most days—that is, when there haven't been too many "decomps," decomposed bodies, brought into the institute—the smell is less than overpowering on the first floor. And most visitors never venture past the first floor.

This level is the home of the bureaucracy of the dead. Beyond the reception room with its spotless bare walls and wooden bench, beyond a glass partition, they work quietly at their desks. Belongings of the deceased are checked in and out. Autopsy records dating back to the foundation of the coroner's office in the 1830s, files and reports, are all housed here in large filing cabinets. East of the reception room is an office full of desks and phones, which the institute's investigators use when they're not in the field, which is where they are most of the time. There is also a small room where families can come to identify bodies via a closed-circuit television system hooked up to a camera in a basement hallway.

After the smell, the most obvious feature of the institute is overcrowding. The quarters here are so cramped that very few of the 124 employees have private offices—and that includes the 11 doctors. Upstairs the situation is no better. The storage shelves in the toxicology lab on the second floor are bursting with specimens—bits of skin, liver, kidney, and brain. Everywhere you turn, every square inch has been used as economically as possible. "We generate so much information that we are not equipped to handle," Dr. Stein has said. The toxicology lab takes up most of the second floor and seems pretty large at first glance, but it shrinks beside the work it only barely houses. Each day specimens from about twenty bodies are brought in for basic chemical and biological work. In addition, data are collected for more complicated research projects; one of the pathologists, for example, regularly examines samples of nerve tissue, looking for clues to the causes of epilepsy. Here disease and its abnormalities are viewed in the rawest state.

Dr. Stein's office is on the second floor across the narrow corridor from the laboratory. Books are packed tightly onto the shelves of the L-shaped room, many of them in sets of two or three or five or twenty. They are about pathology and aspects of law and medicine. For now, Dr. Stein's office is also the institute's library. A long table almost the length of the office holds trays of thousands of slides and a lighted viewer, a small sample of the institute's vast collection. (Slides are made of each body processed here.) Stein frequently lectures to medical students and other groups—he holds a professorial rank at all the Chicago-area medical schools—and he uses slides in his presentations. "It never fails," Dr. Stein says. "There they are at age twenty-three. You have these young men and women who go to all these movies which leave nothing to anyone's imagination, in which all this language is used, in which there is every type of violence, and I always, always say if anybody doesn't like the material that is presented, please feel free to leave. Invariably, I get somebody who says, 'Why are you using scare tactics?' Well, you know the stuff we see here, for goodness sakes. I showed them an eight-year-old youngster who had a sexual relationship with her ten-year-old brother. I showed them the interiors of her genitals. If you're going to do a complete physical examination, you can't miss that. I tell them, you just might see such a thing in your practice."

There is scarcely room for decoration in this office, but there are a few artistic pieces around: Over by the windows, a very young George Dunne looks out from an eight-by-ten black-and-white photograph. On the floor, waiting for wall space, is a large, posterlike color graphic with a drawing of a medical examiner surrounded by scenes of suicide, homicide, industrial accidents, disease. Next to the door the seven dwarfs with pickaxes and lanterns march in line up a hill in a colorful painting. It is quite a nice cartoon, though there are too many sharp edges—the jaws and features of the elves are squared off—for it to be mistaken for Walt Disney. The painting is the original work of John Wayne Gacy. Dr. Stein got it for $45. Another plaque hanging on the wall reads, "Let conversation cease, let laughter flee, this is the place where death delights to help the living."

In the basement, the smell of putrid flesh is a definite presence, just slightly less than stifling. You start breathing through your mouth, and you think about the headache you'd have after a few hours down there. There are bodies, most of them in green plastic bags in long tin pans; they've been wheeled into the corridors on gurneys and parked there, waiting for some stage of processing. It is like the preoperative section of a hospital in the early morning, except here everyone who waits is already dead. The elevator opens onto the autopsy rooms. To the right is a row of refrigerated compartments where more plastic-shrouded bodies are shelved at about thirty-eight degrees. To the left of the elevator is the camera end of the in-house television outfit. If the family is unable to make an identification by TV, this is where they will come for a closer look. Beyond that area there is another cold storage unit known as the Rose Room, where the worst of the decomposed bodies are kept. All of the equipment—with the exception of the video equipment—is old. The door handles on the cold storage rooms have the same heavy, metallic click as the freezer door on an old-fashioned Good Humor truck. Inside, with their shelves and exposed pipes, they look like 1920s-style steambaths.

This is truly an awful place. It makes the morgues in the gangster movies of the '40s look like modern, deluxe facilities. The basement is clean, well lighted, and functional, but you are always aware that it is a basement, old and decrepit. All that is missing is a constant drip, drip, drip from some obscure corner. The decay of the bodies here has been halted. But even the most scrupulous maintenance of the institute has not kept the building from deteriorating beyond the point of no return.

"It was scheduled for demolition the first quarter of 1982," says Roy Dames, Dr. Stein's administrative assistant. "Every day we pray that it's still going to be there when we show up in the morning."

● ● ●

Starting in 1833, the city of Chicago was built rapidly by annexing territory upon little territory to the center of town, that is, to the area of several square blocks around the present site of City Hall and Daley Center. Most of these territories later became neighborhoods: Lakeview, Hyde Park, Bridgeport, and so forth. But one of the first areas, the neighborhood to its immediate west, was "withdrawn by act of legislature" and given over to various low-prestige public buildings. One of the first of these was the morgue. The county's public morgue came into existence about 1840; its function was to keep dead people off the streets. The duties of the official responsible for the morgue were to protect the interests of the government.

The word *coroner* originates from the Latin *corona*, or "crown." In medieval England, the coroner's job was like the job of the bailiff or the sheriff. He was charged with looking out for the king's money, specifically with confiscating the property of murderers, lawbreakers, and suicides—all of which was forfeit to the crown. Over the years the coroner's duties came to include many of the legal (and some of the medical) aspects of death; by the time the office was written into the Illinois constitution in 1870, the disposition of dead people and their effects was a highly developed system.

The first and last real glimpse into the operation of the coroner's office came from Emil Dietzsch, a Cook County coroner who wrote three annual reports in 1874, 1875, and 1876. Mr. Dietzsch was quick to tell the county's 600,000 inhabitants how hard he had worked for his $3,000 annual stipend. In 1874, he presided at 541 inquests—official investigations to determine the cause of death. Each inquest took anywhere from three or four hours to three or four days. He had worked forty-three of fifty-two Sundays, he said; sixty-two inquests were held after 8:00 P.M., and seven of those were after midnight. As if long hours were not enough, Dietzsch went on to emphasize some of the other drawbacks to his job. "Few of my fellow citizens and friends would like to be my constant companion in my daily excursions to all, even the most distant, parts of the county; for they would have to visit the uncleanly hovels of poverty and destitution, as well as the haunts of various forms of social vice. They would have to be hardened against all sorts of sickening impressions, overcome disgust, calmly bear brutality, and keep the even tenor of their way, unmoved by pity or indignation."

There were sixty-nine suicides that year—forty-nine men, two boys, and the rest women—of whom "six cut their throats with razors, seventeen committed suicide by hanging, twenty-five by poisoning, twelve by shooting, and nine by drowning." The second most frequent cause of death that warranted inquest was accidental drowning; Dietzsch reported sixty-two cases. Twelve deaths were due to delirium tremens, seven to elevator accidents. Sixty-one people were killed in railroad accidents, forty-seven died from heart disease, thirty-one from diseases of the brain, eight as a result of explosions, six from epilepsy, seventeen were burnt or scalded, and thirteen infants died from convulsions. "The remaining eighty-four cases resulted from a great variety of causes the most noteworthy among which are the following: One man died in consequence of having been bitten by a tiger. Two persons were suffocated with escaping gas, two children were starved to death, two persons were frozen to death, and in six cases the corpses had previously been interred, and afterwards illegally taken, for the purposes of sending them to the anatomical schools of the country. Three persons died of lock-jaw; and three were victims of abortion; seven died from general debility, one with sunstroke; twenty-one were killed by falling from high buildings; and fifteen by accidents handling machinery. Finally—and I am sorry that in the interest of truth it is not desirable to remain silent on this subject which is a strain upon our public morality—I have to report that within this one year there were found within the city limits not less than twenty-nine corpses of babes, exposed immediately after birth, and twenty-eight hidden in various places. Unfortunately I have reason to believe that at least twice as many of these evidences of crime have escaped the watchful eye of the authorities. . . ."

Dietzsch's history of the coroner's office is loaded with opinions and short commentary as well as statistics. He was definitely in favor of capital punishment and felt that criminals were let off too easily. He showed foresight in calling for the more frequent use of photography and chemical analyses in certain cases, and he cited the instance of an unsolved murder in which one of the prime suspects had blood on his shirt, though it could not be proved that the blood came from the victim. Mr. Dietzsch took great interest in the psychological motivations of the many suicides in his jurisdiction, noting that syphilis was "the most frequent and most secret motive for suicide.

" 'Thymos' (see Plato) is particularly well developed in Germans, and they readily fall victim to psychomachy," he wrote—his meaning being more or less that Germans were high-spirited and that was why they frequently had troubled souls. "Among forty-nine male suicides only one could be found of whom it was actually demonstrated that it was love—disappointed, jilted love—which impelled him to end his miserable existence. Verily the times of Hero and Leander, of Juliet and Romeo, have gone by; unfortunate enthusiasts who die for love's sake have become as rare as comets among the lights of the firmament, and when they do appear, alas! derision is what they meet with more frequently than admiration and poetical glorification. . . .

"Napoleon I is credited with the remark that 'From the sublime to the ridiculous there is but one step.' Let us make the step then, and pass from the contemplation of the tragedy of love to that of the poor fellow who blew out what little brains he had on account of the tortures to which he was daily subjected by his mother-in-law. Mothers-in-law have always been a great power of mischief in the world, and alas! the plague is so universal and enduring that we must despair of ever seeing it overcome. The misery caused by mothers-in-law is eternal, even as mothers-in-law themselves are immortal.''

Emil Dietzsch was the first coroner to publicly make the complaint that would be chronic with the men who succeeded him. "In conclusion, I will say that the condition of the morgue is simply disgusting, and a disgrace to the community.''

By the time the new morgue was built in 1925–26, the coroner's office had grown dramatically—of course, so had the amount of work. Oscar Wolff, the coroner at the time, administered his office from the City-County Building, the fabulous new multimillion-dollar facility on Dearborn Street between Washington and Randolph. Wolff was paid $9,000 in 1925 (the coroner's salary would be decreased later on during the Great Depression); Wolff's chief deputy received $5,000, his chief clerk $3,000, and the morgue keeper $2,016. Deputies were given fees on a monthly basis, ranging from $208 to $300. There were forty-five people on the staff, including seven physicians and five chemists, and they processed about 35,000 deaths. Disease was the most common cause of death during that period. Heart disease killed 6,309, and diarrhea more than 1,000. There were 1,100 suicides and homicides, and three people—Lawrence Washington and Willie Sons (both colored, according to county records) and Frank Lanciano—were legally executed at Cook County Jail.

One prominent Cook County resident who passed away during Oscar Wolff's tenure was the venerable John G. Shedd, chairman of the board of directors of Marshall Field & Company and well-known philanthropist, who died in 1926. He had lived to the ripe old age of seventy-six, and there was no inquest. But by far the most celebrated death of Wolff's term came in the spring of 1925, when Bobby Franks was murdered by Leopold and Loeb.

Oscar Wolff was every newspaper reporter's dream, an endless source of speculation about the sensational murder. In an interview with the *Chicago Tribune,* he said: "They must have been educated to have drafted that ransom letter in such perfect English. That would signify intelligence, a dangerous attribute in a criminal, and [might] render him devoid of either conscience or the ability to feel remorse. Greed would be the controlling passion and, dead or alive, they intended to cash in on the millionaire's son.'' He went on to tell the press that he believed the killer was familiar with the area where the body was found and that a Hegewisch disorderly house was being checked out because "If the killer is a degenerate, he may have frequented the house I have in mind." Wolff theorized that the kidnappers had accidentally killed Franks in the struggle to capture him, but decided to collect the ransom money anyway.

● ● ●

For the next twenty-five years the budget and staff of the Cook County Coroner gradually increased while the reputation of the office declined. The coroner was subject to all kinds of political pressure and manipulation; it was known that inquests were fixed and that you could get away with murder. In the '50s it was first suggested that the county abolish the elected office of coroner and adopt the medical examiner, first introduced in Massachusetts in 1880. Under this system, a physician who was also a licensed forensic pathologist was appointed to head an independent investigative agency. By the 1950s many larger communities had switched over, but in Illinois the plan was opposed by the Illinois Coroners Association and the downstate counties: the coroners did not want to give up political power; the downstate counties said they couldn't afford it.

In 1960, Andrew J. Toman, only the third doctor to be elected coroner in Cook County history, took office. Although Dr. Toman, who went on to serve three more consecutive terms, is generally given credit for the abolition of the office (he ran for reelection on the issue in 1972) and for upgrading the facilities and standards while it existed, there were several incidents that demonstrated the need for an autonomous medical chief. It was Toman's office that backed up the story of State's Attorney Edward Hanrahan that Chicago police officers had killed Black Panther leaders Fred Hampton and Mark Clark in self-defense. Years later it was proven in court that accurate autopsy evidence would have shown the police version to be false.

Pressure for change was mounting in 1970, when the Illinois Constitutional Convention met. Though the push to mandate a professional office failed, a compromise was effected. Article 7, Section 4, of the new constitution provided that "Each county shall elect a sheriff, county clerk, and a treasurer and may elect or appoint a coroner," meaning Cook County could switch to the medical examiner system if that is what Cook County wanted to do. That same year saw the publication of a damning study, "An Inquest on the Cook County Coroner," by Richard P. Fahey of the Law

Enforcement Study Group and Deborah J. Palmer of Northwestern University Law School. The study examined a number of inquests at close range and found the system wanting. There were questions on the propriety of jury selection procedures: of 23,000 jury openings, all were filled by men in their late 50s to early 90s, worse, 70 individuals accounted for 906 jury seats (the inference was that coroner's juries were stacked with Democratic party hacks). The report further stated that no inquest took more than forty-five minutes and that the policeman's version of the death was normally the only version presented. The report suggested that the office's $850,000 appropriation was mishandled. While enormous sums were spent on patronage jurors, there were only seventy-seven people working in the office. The coroner himself was paid only about $25,000, and the director of pathology received $30,000. Both salaries were far below the average income of a practicing physician.

In 1972, Dr. Toman was elected for the last time and the coroner's office was legislated out of existence, effective in 1976, the end of Toman's term.

The Cook County Board of Commissioners appointed Dr. Stein, who had been the chief pathologist in the coroner's office, to the $65,000-a-year post of medical examiner in September 1976. He took over the following December. Soon afterward he went before the county board and told them, among other things, that the place was "too small, dreary, dank, crumbling, and rat-infested."

On August 9, 1979, Stein took a specially engraved shovel and scooped out the first bit of earth from the site where one day there would be a $12-million facility for the disposal of the dead and the benefit of the living.

● ● ●

By now you must know Dr. Robert J. Stein, the first medical examiner of Cook County. You have seen him on television and in the newspapers. He is one of the most visible of public servants. He is popular. There are politicians who would love to get the exposure he gets. Robert Stein is a likable guy with many of the qualities of a family doctor. He says he is in his early sixties. His gray hair is neatly coiffed, and his eyes sparkle from behind his glasses. He has a warm smile and a good sense of humor. He is businesslike but loves to make conversation. He is frank but not intimidating. He seems like

Someone else might say, 'No, I disagree.' That's the way it goes. So it's not the decision of one person out of this office. No one else has any input whatsoever. None. Zero. Nothing.''

At 8:30 sharp, Stein begins making rounds. From his secretary, Joana Krutulis, he picks up a handful of typed sheets listing the bodies and their histories and returns to the basement.

This is a very, very unusual morning, the first morning like it in many years. There are only five cases on this list, instead of the usual twenty or more. Four pathologists are standing around in the hallways near one of the bodies when Stein arrives, but the group soon includes medical technicians, and the herd grows and the rounds continue. Dr. Lee Beamer, a tall man with dark hair and a beard, is the pathologist of the day, and he reads off the list. As it happens, there are only a couple of bodies to look at: a forty-one-year-old black male and a seventy-nine-year-old Caucasian male. The rest haven't arrived yet from the place of death. The seventy-nine-year-old is the more interesting one. The man, who has been missing his right arm for a long time, has committed suicide by shooting himself in the head. "We're seeing more and more of these old people committing suicide," Stein points out. Of course, the doctors and the technicians are used to seeing dead people, and the examination tour does not faze them a bit. But even for a lay person, making rounds is not a horrifying experience; corpses look much more like mannequins than like human beings. Once the bodies have been displayed, the pathologists give the details on the bodies that have not yet arrived.

Dr. Joann Richmond, a pretty woman in her thirties with delicate features, tells the story of a white female, also a doctor and about the same age, who died during the night on the southwest side of a possible overdose. The dead woman's mother said that around midnight her daughter came into her bedroom and lay down beside her on the bed, saying she had had a bad dream. At about 1:30 the mother heard her daughter talking on the phone, asked whom she was talking to, and was told her girlfriend. Later, when the mother went to check on the daughter, she found her unresponsive on the bed. The daughter was taken to a private hospital, where she was classified as a polydrug overdose. Empty pill bottles were found in her room. The deceased had been treated at Forest Hospital a month earlier for a drug overdose. The dead woman will be donating her eyes, so Stein starts a brief discussion on what organs can and cannot be donated in the case of a drug overdose. The pathologists agree that it will be all right to take the dead doctor's eyes.

There follows the long, sad story of a thirty-nine-year-old female, told by a small, dark, woman physician, Dr. Shaku Teas. The dead woman was retarded and had been in and out of many institutions. For the last few years she had spent most of the time in the custody of her brother-in-law, though the public guardian took her away from him for a while when it was suspected that she was being abused. After a few months she was returned to the brother-in-law and had since been visited by a nurse and occasionally a doctor. The brother-in-law had described her as self-destructive, and she had been made to wear a steel helmet to protect her from falls. The brother-in-law complained that prior to January 5, she had been refusing to eat. According to the report, her body shows fractures and bruises.

Dr. Barry Lifschultz, who has glasses and curly hair and seems almost too young to be a doctor, has a set of Polaroid pictures made by the medical investigators of the body of a sixty-six-year-old black male who was found by his sister in the Chicago Heights apartment where he lived alone. The water in his apartment was shut off, and he was apparently using a propane torch to fix an overhead water pipe when his clothing caught fire. When the sister discovered his body, the torch was still turned on, though it was out of gas, and the two burners on the stove were lit. The man, who was retired, often worked around the house and had a history of a heart condition and sickle-cell anemia. Dr. Stein instructs Dr. Lifschultz as to what is needed when the body comes in.

On his way back to his office Stein stops to tell one of the technicians that he is looking pretty good. The technician says that he has knocked off about thirty-two pounds. Stein says that he has knocked off twenty himself.

"Somebody doing your life story, doctor?" The technician points to me.

"Only my sex life," Stein says.

• • •

Dr. Stein has been to court three times this week, so by Friday afternoon he has a lot on his mind, and most of it has to do with law and medicine. The two things, Dr. Stein will tell you, do not mix. "There's a big, big interface between medicine and law, and there's something I quote to my students and everybody. It's like when this young attorney confronted Oliver Wendell Holmes and Holmes said, 'Remember as long as you practice, this is a court of law and not of justice,' " One of Stein's cases this week involved the delicate question of suicide—a problem mostly because of insurance policies that will not pay when the deceased has taken his own life. Suicide, Stein explains, depends on the intent of the victim: if he didn't intend to kill himself, it wasn't suicide. But if the victim *did* intend to kill himself, then he is not of sound mind, and if he is not of sound mind, then he couldn't have made up his unsound mind to do something. Intent becomes invalid. So, Stein says, a real legalist will tell you that there is no such thing as suicide. The issue gets even muddier if you add drugs and/or alcohol to the picture. Stein mentions the case of Freddie Prinze: because there were drugs in his system when he shot himself, the court ordered an insurance company to pay a settlement to Prinze's mother. "So therefore, somebody shoots himself, leaves a suicide note and everything, it's called a suicide. And you go to court and the lawyers say, uh-uh-uh, no-no, that person is not of sound mind."

This kind of stuff drives Dr. Stein crazy, these lawyers treading all over his turf. "What I don't understand—and I grant you it's done daily—is why in court you have legal minds overruling medical opinion. If someone were to practice medicine without license, they'd be put in jail or fined or something. I'm not practicing law." Dr. Stein has a tendency to stretch his vowels when he gets emotional and wants to make a point. You could have placed a short phone call during these last two vowels, and he is just getting warmed up.

Let's go back to the beginning. Forget homicide, suicide, accident. what about the definition of death? There's a thorny point for medical examiners and lawyers to argue about. "I know that our life is controlled by laws; it has to be," Stein says. "But when you're going to say it's the bench that decides whether or not you're going to remove someone from a life-support system, I say no. I feel that this is entirely up to the family and their own family physician. Not the authorities. The bench feels very uneasy about it, anyway. There's just no doubt in my mind. The authorities have no right."

Yesterday Stein testified for Loyola Medical Center. "What happened in this Loyola case was, on September 29, they bring this seven-, eight-week-old baby in with a head injury and put it on a respirator. Just at that time there was an appeal by a father in New

York at a pediatrics society convention for a liver. This baby on the respirator was the perfect candidate. So at Loyola they were going to pull the plug. But the parents say no, and they get an attorney. The state's attorney's office calls me and says, 'Dr. Stein, what's your definition of death?' and I said very simply it's the Harvard committee plus the AMA guidelines, anatomic uniform act—Illinois does not have a strict definition of death—there is flat EEG, the brain circulation is all gone, the same as everybody else in the world. OK, so, I have to go to court yesterday and testify. It's a bench trial, and this attorney who is eighty-two years of age calls me a murderer. Well, I like that because, in a situation like this, where I'm being called a murderer, if I'm able to save some human being's life, then you call me any damn thing you want."

Besides raising the death issue, the Loyola case brings up another of Dr. Stein's favorite topics, the rights of a society to organs for transplant operations. "I am absolutely pathologic on this subject," Stein says. "My son's friend is in his second year of law school now. When he was a kid, he was nothing by nothing. The other kids protected the boy because he was so tiny. I said at the time, 'Why don't you get in touch with so-and-so at Mayo Clinic? They have experimental pituitary extract. Get the injection of the growth hormone.' The kid shot up. He's normal height now, five feet, seven inches. It's wonderful, and if he didn't get that hormone, he would be five foot tall. Think of the mental trauma. Let's say out of 4,000 autopsies we do here we get 2,000 pituitaries. We could have so many!

"If I get a call here about removing the cornea of an eye, I have to get permission of the family to do that. I respect that. But must you always get permission of the family? The funeral directors put in eye cups anyway, nobody ever sees the eyes. They're all closed. If you remove the eyes, so what? And the kidneys. With kidneys there's a very, very critical time factor. At least with eye cornea there's a good six hours, maybe twelve hours. Skin—we have this burn unit here at the hospital. They need skin. If there's a strong religious thing with the family and they don't want to do it, I can understand that; we all would. The thing I can't understand is when you have a young man with a long police record. The young man is shot, a confrontation in a crap game or something. He's dead. Now here comes the family. They couldn't have cared less about the young man, but now he's such a good, wonderful boy."

Or take the case of a family that cannot be located. The medical examiner takes the liver and puts it in a plastic bag and buries the body. All of a sudden the family comes around with an attorney and files a lawsuit. There is something wrong with this scenario as far as Stein is concerned. For years he has been pursuing legislation making it all right to take organs from the deceased when they are needed and the next of kin is not around. The Illinois Anatomical Gift Act says that a person can decide to contribute his body to science effective at the time of death or that the next of kin may make such a decision, but there is a strict priority as to next of kin, and the list is eight people long. By law, Stein is the authorized person if no next of kin can be established, but he has been seeking a stronger law in the form of a county ordinance to give him greater authority and protect him from liability. The Cook County Board hasn't come around yet: last year's county ordinance on cornea removal is probably stricter in practice than the state law.

• • •

"What interested me most about the Gacy case was the background of the kids, the families. I was just floored. The people wouldn't come here to make identification. Then they wouldn't pick up the body for a month or longer. Did you see the pictures of the burial of the unidentified victims? Nine separate hearses. Flowers, all that stuff. I thought the funeral directors of the city of Chicago did a tremendous job, a tremendous job. I said, 'We'll see, maybe the parents will show up at the funeral or something.' But we never saw them. Not a soul. Not a soul.

"You know what bothers me? This violence as a way of life. You know very well if you put two mice in a cage they get along famously. You put another one in, and they are fighting for food. They're fighting for sex, a mate. This whole business of violence . . . . Well, let's put it this way: I think all of us are inherently violent. But I think because of our upbringing, perhaps because of our environment, or circumstances, we don't act out our violence. Here's something I hold very, very dear: the family structure. If you have a good family and good parents, you're not violent. You might poke somebody in the nose, or get in a fistfight as a child, but to go to the extremes to produce the death of an individual! What you see here which I had never seen years ago is—years ago you would shoot somebody once; now they empty the whole barrel. They shoot somebody a dozen times.

"The things that change are the weapons, the violence. In the old days a guy would take an ax, or a club, and that was it. Clobber somebody over the head with a baseball bat once. Okay, stop. Now they dismember them. They remove their arms and legs. Like this torso that was found the other day. They removed the head, removed both arms, removed both legs including the pelvis, and the guy had been shot through the heart! That was like this case I had here where the guy had the arms and legs of his beloved one and he sent the head to the Philippines. He's rehabilitated now. I don't understand. That's the point.

"The real life is right here. It's the violence. The violence in all of us. Charles Darwin said, 'It's the struggle for existence and the survival of the fittest.' Why do you have wars? Why do you compete in your job? I'm a very, very firm believer in the Darwinian theory of natural selection.

"We had a case where the people had been strangled and shot, but what intrigued me about it was you went into the house and the kids were bitten to bits by cockroaches. Rat bites. That's what intrigues me. How do human beings live in such squalor? The big thing is drug-associated death. But why was that drug-associated? Why was that drug there? What kind of life is that? That's the point. That's what people don't see. This is not newsworthy. A dead fifteen-year-old child, a young lady—she's been a hooker since she was twelve. That's what's tragic. Bodies found underneath the bed with the cockroaches. That body never had a life. You find yourself really thinking about the quality of life.

"You see, I remember as a young boy the Great Depression. I remember we lived up in the Bronx in a gorgeous (by those standards) five-room apartment. My father lost everything we had, and we moved into one room. There were other families there. There was one kitchen and one john. The thing I recall so vividly was people hanging themselves. Selling apples, I saw that. Soup lines, I saw that. Then when I read now what's happening in California and some other places. They have these so-called tent cities. It's just a tent or buildings made out of scrap metal. People living in cars.

"I see a lot of suicide among the very, very old now. Speaking of child abuse, how about grandma and grandpa abuse? The children just don't want them. You know that's very, very heartbreaking and very depressing, but you just can't help it. That brings up the question of euthanasia, which is something I refuse to even discuss.

"These are the things that bug me. When I drive home I always talk to myself. I argue with myself. When I get home I have a manhattan and I get tranquilized."

• • •

The way he sees it, Dr. Stein has three main problems: money, politics, and the media. He characterizes them as "show business." He wishes he had a bigger staff and a larger budget, but his job, he says, is to manage with what he's got. Two bright spots are that he has eleven pathologists; more than any other medical examiner's office in the country, and that his staff will soon be quartered in one of the finest facilities of its kind in the world.

One of the frequent complaints against the medical examiner's office is that it takes too much time for a case to get signed out. "Look, you have what is known as polypharmacy," Stein explains. "You don't have just one drug in the body. You have a combination of different drugs. In the old days it was one drug. It was easy. Now the attorneys will tell you they're only interested in big things. *Garbage!* They will want to know why the *I* wasn't dotted or the *T* wasn't crossed. When you do a polypharmacy you have traces of this compound, of this compound, of this compound. Each in itself is lethal. So you have to decide. Of course, people are not getting reports rapidly. Of course they're unhappy.

"The one thing which I'm very, very conscious of is that we are a tax-supported facility, damn it. You have to watch the taxpayer's dollar. You can't just go before George Dunne and ask for money. What you've got to do, by golly, is really get your ass moving, be more efficient, spend more time, period.

"We've got twenty investigators. The investigators are lay investigators. They go to the scene. They gather information for the doctors that the police might not have. Sometimes the police will gather information that we do not have. Therefore, we kind of complement each other. Ten percent of the deaths here are unexplained. Nobody knows anything, and this takes a lot of time. This is where you've got to dig and dig and dig. I always say our investigators are the backbone of the pathologists. What kind of training do they have? They have nothing. They get the training here. Many of them are funeral directors. Some of them were in service. A number of the investigators are strictly patronage jobs. However, I do have the right to turn them down. Over 95 percent of the people recommended from downtown I turn down. They fill out application forms, and I see exactly how they write and how they spell. They've got to be minimum high school graduate. I like to see their school transcript. My interest is in one grade—math. The reason is logic. They have to be able to think.

●   ●   ●

"We are emerging from the dark ages of the coroner's office."

Part of coming out has meant opening the medical examiner's office to close scrutiny, and close scrutiny has meant lots of media around all the time and some criticism from the press. Stein has been accused of seeking stardom and keeping too high a profile, charges he dismisses as nonsense. That kind of allegation seems to be a professional hazard with medical examiners. Stein's counterpart in Los Angeles, Dr. Tom Noguchi, was recently ousted, reinstated, then ousted again, partly on account of his statements to the media. "Let's go to William Holden," Stein says. "Tom said this much alcohol was found, combined with the laceration he had on his head, he fell against a chest of drawers. That's exactly what happened. So they told him, 'Don't say anything about the cause of death. You shouldn't say anything more.' Well, that's ridiculous because when we testify in court we have to go on and on and on, because they don't understand."

The "they" in Stein's career is the media. There have been some misunderstandings in Cook County, though they have been nowhere as serious as those in Los Angeles.

Unwarranted criticism is a fact of life for medical examiners.

Of course, real mistakes have been made in Dr. Stein's office. He is the first to admit that. Last March, it was discovered that the bodies of two victims of a north-side hotel fire had been mixed up. One of Stein's investigators had to be suspended in October when he ruled that a west-side woman had died of natural causes. An embalmer noticed stab wounds, and the death was declared a homicide. The matter was investigated, and the employee served the suspension and was retained.

"Are errors made?" Stein says. "Oh, sure, it's human. We do make errors here. Do we admit it? Of course, we admit it. Hopefully we're human here, too. Hopefully."

●   ●   ●

Allen Dorfman may turn out to be the last important corpse to get its toe tag at the tumbledown Fishbein Institute. If you and I survive for the next few weeks or so, we can be pretty sure that, should we die an unnatural death or should our bodies be found on the street, we will end up in the careful hands of the county pathologists at the most magnificent "morgue" (although it will never be called by that name in Dr. Stein's presence) in the entire world, the new Cook County Institute of Forensic Medicine. It was designed by architect Andrew Heard with Dr. Stein's specifications in mind, and, except for the autopsy rooms and the cold storage unit almost the size of a football field (equipped to handle any disaster), you might mistake the place for a small, well-appointed school.

The ambulance that might bring your body here, taking either Harrison or Polk, will turn on to Hamilton and the rear entrance used for body delivery and nighttime business. There are mirrored windows here so that the security guard at the communications center just inside the back door can get a good look at visitors before they get a look at him.

If your body is not too badly decomposed, your remains will be unloaded onto a tray coated with a Teflonlike substance mounted on a stainless steel cart specially designed to hold the tray and to be raised or lowered to the height most comfortable for the pathologist. They were made to order for Dr. Stein by the Jewett Company.

You will be wheeled straight into the main cooling section, and some preliminary work, like weighing in, will be done before you are transferred from the cart onto one of the 200 slots built in tiers across the room. You will stay there until it is time for the pathologist of the day to take a look at you.

Had you come here badly decomposed, you would have been brought through a different, separate garage-type door and hooked up on a monorail so that no technician would have to lift you up. By keeping the entrance, ventilation, and workrooms of the decomps separate, it is thought that there will be no odor in the new buildings. After you have been weighed and checked in, you will be placed inside your own refrigerator or freezer compartment with its own little door. After you are tucked away, the area will be cleaned with high-powered hoses attached to the wall of the autopsy rooms, which spray water and a water-detergent mixture.

Meanwhile, the police who brought you in will be talking to the medical investigators and other personnel who will have done the field work in your case. The investigators will have their own cubicles with desks and phones. If it is the middle of the night, your effects will be placed in the night depository and the custodian will check them in the next morning. Your belongings will be very secure, because the alarm system in the building has been put together with great care and the safe, which is the size of a small closet, is made of concrete and steel.

• • •

If it is decided that you need an autopsy, you will be taken to one of the autopsy rooms south of the big refrigerator. If space is at a premium for some reason, the operation might be done at a work area with a sink. Some cases will go to a special autopsy room with a closed-circuit camera hooked up to the big conference room downstairs. As many as 200 people can watch an autopsy from the conference room, where there are several large screens and a black-board for audiovisual presentations. The equipment can be operated from a wood-paneled booth in the rear of the room or a duplicate panel at the podium. Along the north wall of the conference room there are skylights that shine down on glass cases that will someday house a small museum.

Back on the first floor there is an X-ray room and a brain cutting room. After your remains have been processed, they will be returned to their stall for pickup and the specimens will be sent via dumb-waiter upstairs to the toxicology lab.

Family members will come in the main entrance on the east side of the building. They will see beautiful carpeting and furniture, a high ceiling, and a large skylight. If an identification is to be made, they will be ushered into a comfortable room off the reception area where they can look at you on closed-circuit television. If a closer look is required, a small area of the refrigerated room can be partitioned off with a curtain so the family can see you through a window. They will probably be surprised to find out that you're so close by.

Near the autopsy rooms are lockers and black-tiled shower stalls where the doctors and technicians can clean up. After that they can go downstairs, next door to the conference room, where there will be vending machines with food and drinks, and they can relax.

On the second floor, the toxicology lab is twice the size of Fishbein's, and there are smaller labs with all the latest equipment. And there are offices up there, for Dr. Stein and Joana Krutulis, for Roy Dames, for the doctors and the lab people, for quite a number of people who have never before had offices. And there is also something entirely new to the Cook County Medical Examiner's Office: storage space and room for expansion.

After your case is processed and you are long gone, your file will be completed and put away in one of the long metal cabinets on the ground floor. There is space for a computer but no plan for installing a system in the immediate future. Improvements have traditionally come slowly to this office.

This place took twice as long as it should have to build, and right now nobody is sure exactly how much it will cost. "Let's put it this way," says Roy. "I hope they don't take it out of our paychecks."

This is really something to be proud of, and you can tell Dr. Stein feels good about it. "There's new history to be made here," he says.

It is everything it should be. It is magnificent. It is impressive, and I tell him that. He says there'll be somebody bitching.

● ● ●

Any day the old Cook County morgue is going to be vacated. It will be torn right down to the ground and carted away just like John Gacy's house. After a while, nobody will remember that there was ever such a place at all.